If you exhibit any of the following symptoms . . .

- Having outbursts of anger out of proportion to the cause
- Repeating behaviors you don't like in spite of your determination not to
- Feeling profoundly exhausted when you're rested
- Repeatedly dating or marrying the wrong person
- Being unable to hold on to a job
- Never being happy with your work
- Thinking that if you just change something about yourself—make more money, lose weight, stop drinking—all your problems will be solved
- Believing that if you just find that right someone, everything else will be fine

. . . then *Becoming Real* is for you.

"Gail Saltz has written a wonderful book that is important, interesting, and fun to read. A must for everyone who wants the most out of life."

—Harold S. Koplewicz, M.D.,
director of the NYU Child Study Center and author of *More than Moody: Recognizing and Treating Adolescent Depression*

"Gail Saltz brings to life her deep understanding of the human condition. A profound and valuable book."   —Newell Fischer, M.D.,
president, American Psychoanalytic Association

"Dr. Gail Saltz challenges each of us to explore the stories we tell ourselves to explain who we are, account for our behavior, and deal with pain and fear. While necessary for our psychological survival, if left unexamined, these stories can limit seriously our capacity for living and loving. This remarkable work speaks in plain language to everyone engaged in the ongoing struggle to live more fully and authentically."   —Jack D. Barchas, M.D.,
chairman of psychiatry at Weill Cornell

"Saltz . . . provides a guide to a kind of narrative unconscious as it affects decision making . . . the author's instructions for undergoing this process are specific and clear."   —*Publishers Weekly*

"We can all learn from her sagacity."   —Tom Brokaw

BECOMING

Defeating the Stories We Tell Ourselves That Hold Us Back

REAL

Gail Saltz, M.D.

Riverhead Books

New York

THE BERKLEY PUBLISHING GROUP
Published by the Penguin Group
Penguin Group (USA) Inc.
375 Hudson Street, New York, New York 10014, USA
Penguin Group (Canada), 10 Alcorn Avenue, Toronto, Ontario M4V 3B2, Canada (a division of Pearson
Penguin Canada Inc.)
Penguin Books Ltd., 80 Strand, London WC2R 0RL, England
Penguin Group Ireland, 25 St. Stephen's Green, Dublin 2, Ireland (a division of Penguin Books Ltd.)
Penguin Group (Australia), 250 Camberwell Road, Camberwell, Victoria 3124, Australia (a division of
Pearson Australia Group Pty. Ltd.)
Penguin Books India Pvt. Ltd., 11 Community Centre, Panchsheel Park, New Delhi—110 017, India
Penguin Group (NZ), Cnr. Airborne and Rosedale Roads, Albany, Auckland 1310, New Zealand (a di-
vision of Pearson New Zealand Ltd.)
Penguin Books (South Africa) (Pty.) Ltd., 24 Sturdee Avenue, Rosebank, Johannesburg 2196, South
Africa

Penguin Books Ltd., Registered Offices: 80 Strand, London WC2R 0RL, England

Names and identifying information of people depicted in this book have been changed to protect their
privacy.

Every effort has been made to ensure that the information contained in this book is complete and accu-
rate. However, neither the publisher nor the author is engaged in rendering professional advice or serv-
ices to the individual reader. The ideas, procedures, and suggestions contained in this book are not
intended as a substitute for consulting with your physician. All matters regarding health require medical
supervision. Neither the author nor the publisher shall be liable or responsible for any loss, injury, or
damage allegedly arising from any information or suggestion in this book.

PRINTING HISTORY
First Riverhead hardcover edition: May 2004
First Riverhead trade paperback edition: May 2005
Riverhead trade paperback ISBN: 1-59448-082-6

The Library of Congress has catalogued the Riverhead hardcover edition as follows:

Saltz, Gail.
Becoming real : defeating the stories we tell ourselves
that hold us back / by Gail Saltz.
p.   cm.
Includes index.
ISBN 1-57322-279-8
1. Self-actualization (Psychology)   2. Self-defeating behavior.   3. Schemas
(Psychology)   I. Title.
BF637.S4S245   2004   2003066887
158.1—dc22

PRINTED IN THE UNITED STATES OF AMERICA

10   9   8   7   6   5   4   3   2   1

TO MY INCREDIBLY LOVING HUSBAND, LENNY,

AND OUR THREE WONDERFUL DAUGHTERS,

EMILY, KIMBERLY, AND VICTORIA

CONTENTS

INTRODUCTION

Life is a gift. It can also be a tremendous struggle. Too many of us wake up every morning anticipating another day of trudging up a giant hill dotted with obstacles, only to go home, go to bed, sleep (or not), and start the cycle all over again. In times like this, we find it hard to enjoy life or make the most out of the gifts we've been given. But we do have a choice. We can see life's struggles as something to avoid at all costs—or we can recognize that struggles are inevitable and choose to approach them as something that can be truly life enhancing, adding to life's intricacy, fascination, creativity, and exhilaration.

There are times we all feel trapped in an unfulfilling cycle, like a hamster, endlessly spinning on a wheel. During these episodes we often feel down or frustrated and unable to figure out what changes to make or how to make them. We spend a lot of time imagining scenarios that would make us happy, but we seem unable to find a path to take us there. We seem to be living out one lousy relationship after another in work or love, never finding any of them satisfying.

If contentment, self-confidence, joy, freedom, and peace elude you and you feel something is blocking you from love and fulfillment, you're probably right. If life always feels unfair and it seems you're always getting the short end of the stick, then you need to seek out what's causing your frustration. It's there, I promise you. It's not a hex, a curse, or a conspiracy. And as hard as it may be to accept, it's not anyone's fault. It's something deep inside every one of us, something that invisibly governs and directs all our lives—it's your own deeply embedded story and it has the ability to shape almost everything about you.

We all have stories, ones that begin at the earliest moments of our lives. Our stories tell us who we are and how the world operates. We create these stories out of necessity. They explain events in our lives that are traumatic and difficult, and they allowed us to hold on to those we loved when they either did not or could not respond to our most essential need to be loved and recognized. These stories have rules, they have dramas, and they have limits. They helped us make sense of our worlds and they provided safety and order. But they also exact a price. They distort our vision and hide our authenticity under their plotlines. We trade much of our essential selves for the false promise our stories make that they will keep us safe and loved.

As we become adults, the true nature of what we've traded becomes evident because, sooner or later, we arrive at a point where we feel emotionally, physically, or spiritually stuck. We feel powerless to make the changes we think would make us happy. Our stories no longer keep us safe; instead they have trapped us. If we want to break destructive patterns, find the intimacy, satisfaction, and recognition we desire, we first have to find out what these stories are and what they tell us about ourselves. This is extremely difficult because they live in our unconscious minds and are thus invisible to us. They masquerade as "truth." They whisper that they are protecting us from the pains of abandonment and rejection. And maybe they did for a while. But as adults they keep us from becoming real.

What do I mean by "real"? Being real means experiencing life's gifts to their fullest. It means being authentic, strong, rooted. It means that along with the pains of loss, we get to experience the joys of closeness, connection, and intimacy. When we're real, we're no longer like tumbleweeds blown around where the wind blows. We have the strength, the stamina, the courage, the power, and the freedom to go where we want to go. Being real means we can tolerate life's discomforts and ambiguities because we are strong enough to embrace the good and the bad, the black, white, and grays of most situations. When we accept this truth, we will become like trees with deep roots—strong and capable and able to weather whatever comes our way. Being real means experiencing the full spectrum of human emotions.

Every day I work with people who come to my office because they just want to feel better. They don't know the cause of their feelings—they just know they are suffering. Even so, patients often have reservations about asking for help. As accepted as psychotherapy has become in our culture, many people still think they have to be in a really bad way before they can consult a mental health professional. This is a tremendous shame because suffering is suffering. It doesn't matter if it's caused by neurotransmitters that affect the brain (as in schizophrenia) or whether it's a pattern of being or thinking that interrupts and prevents them from getting the most out of each day. It's still suffering.

Much of what I do centers on helping my patients understand this suffering precisely because it's by following the paths of people's pain and depression that they ultimately begin to understand their stories and get the chance to rewrite them. This process can be messy, I tell them, and they can't have what they want without feeling some real discomfort. Since we are almost never told the truth—that living life brings inevitable pain—we think that each time we experience pain that it is proof something's wrong with us. Since we don't want to feel even worse about ourselves, we try to avoid emotional pain with all our might, not recognizing that pain often holds the key to our awakening and happiness.

Whenever we experience an unpleasant feeling, rather than going right into it and seeing it as a part of life, our society has taught us to see it as something to avoid, eliminate, or suppress. For the last few decades, we've been offered a palette of self-gratifying shortcuts. We can take a pill, buy a new lipstick, or check out a new diet or relationship book. All of these promise us that we can be new and improved. We can have lots of gain with no pain. It is an understandable wish—who wouldn't want that?

But these shortcuts don't work. They don't work because they are neat external solutions to inner problems. They seek to avoid pain without confronting its source. It's like putting a Band-Aid on a deep wound without cleaning it out so it can properly heal. Being human, we look to avoid pain, but when we do, we lose the opportunity to follow the pain to the deepest part of our unconscious minds where our stories sit, spinning their magic about what does and doesn't make us lovable, adequate, or acceptable. But it's only when we make the decision to go into these deep places that we reap the reward of breaking free from the old, restricting narratives we have long outgrown.

One of the reasons I have written this book is that in this day and age of advancing psychopharmacology and the various cognitive therapies, we have lost sight of the existence and the power of the unconscious. It's been the trend to focus on our chemistry or biology or on therapies that are about what's going on in our conscious mind and how we can alter them. I have nothing against these therapies—they can be extremely useful—and I'm a believer in medication for the right people at the right time and under the right therapeutic conditions. But I also know how tremendously powerful the unconscious mind is. In some ways, it's more powerful than our conscious minds because we don't easily see the tendrils it shoots out and the stories it creates. We don't see how those stories make us think, behave, and feel in certain ways. When we dismiss or diminish the power of the unconscious, it is like operating with our hands tied behind our backs.

I don't underestimate how difficult it is for anyone to seek help. So many people feel ashamed—they feel that if they need therapy, there must be something terribly wrong with them; they fear they are really truly crazy or unbalanced deep inside. But in my experience, this fear is 99.9% unjustified. Others think seeking help makes them "self-centered," which has become such a dirty word. This, too, is a shame because I believe one of the most important things to achieve in life is self-appreciation and self-loving. If we truly love ourselves, we are the opposite of self-centered. We will not need to focus on ourselves and our needs all the time, and we will be free to look around and love others. We will have the energy and drive to give love, empathy, and understanding because we are not being sucked dry by constant activity aimed at covering up how much we don't like ourselves. I tell my patients that one of the most generous acts of their lives can be doing the work of learning what it is—what story—keeps them from truly liking and loving themselves. Because until they understand the story's silent instructions, contentment, peace, and freedom will likely elude them, making it impossible to appreciate life's gifts and share them with others.

While it is true that it is hard to teach an old dog new tricks, human beings are amazingly malleable. We are always capable of change. And though there are infinite numbers of individuals—making a cookie-cutter recipe for change impossible—there are general themes we all share that run through our lives. It is my hope that this book will help you understand the general principles of how we develop and what made us who we are today. Throughout this book, I will give you tools to help you see how your personality was formed and how you've learned to protect both your character and your story—even without your knowledge. You will also get the instruments you need to help you make the changes that can free you from years of living a fiction.

I hope that when you read this book, you will see and understand not only parts of yourself but parts of your loved ones, too. Maybe what you learn here will help you clue in your spouse or parent. Perhaps you'll be able to help them see that they, too, have stories that leave them stuck in some place that they just can't seem to move beyond. Maybe you will be able to forgive yourself and them as you realize that you and they are not at fault.

We all create stories to explain the events in our lives that felt traumatic or even just very difficult. They can start as a result of a

huge tragedy like losing a parent or child abuse; this kind of inter-
ruption can make you afraid of getting close to anyone and irrationally make you hate yourself for being so bad that you deserved to
be left or abused. However, a story can be formed by something as
mundane as stumbling across your naked father in the bathroom when
you're eight and feeling naturally curious yet conflicted about it. The
story that results from this can be that curiosity itself is a bad thing,
and this can have lifelong damaging repercussions when not understood.

I particularly wanted to write this book now in this day and age, as
insurance companies, looking for faster and cheaper treatments, have
escalated the use of medications, cognitive behavioral therapies, and
quick fixes that try to bypass the unconscious, where these stories
grow and mutate. While there are advantages to many of these prac-
tices and their use may be helpful or necessary at various times, without some understanding of the power of the unconscious—without
some understanding of how we became who we are and what our core
conflicts and dynamics are—we can't change the underlying issues that
may continue to precipitate depression, anxiety, and that feeling of being stuck in a miserable life. I'm not saying don't take the drugs. I'm
saying that without understanding who we are and how we came to
be the way we are, the likelihood of staying stuck and repeating the
same destructive, distancing, unfulfilling, and frustrating patterns is
extremely high.

This book does not contain a simple three-step program that will
change your life, make you rich, give you great sex, take off those
twenty pounds you're carrying, and give you the winning lottery
numbers for SuperLotto. What it will do is show you—gently and

carefully—how and why the person you have become is only a fraction of the real you. When we have a road map to delve into our unconscious mind where our stories dwell, we arrive at a destination that is richer and fuller than anything we let ourselves imagine. This book contains that map.

Chapter One

THE POWER OF
WHAT WE DON'T KNOW

Sydney is a long-legged, striking woman in her early thirties. She has beautiful brown hair, cut so it swings when she talks with great animation—which is most of the time. She is upbeat and charming and has an infectious laugh. She's curious and sweet and clearly wants to set everyone at ease. These skills have served her well in what has become a very successful marketing career. On top of all that, Sydney has tons of girlfriends and is engaged to a man who is clearly crazy about her.

So, why is she on the brink of blowing everything up? As her wedding day draws near, she's become distant, cold, and angry at her fiancé, Brian. He keeps asking her if something's wrong, but Sydney denies there's a problem, insisting everything is okay. But he feels like the woman he fell in love with has been replaced by this volatile, erratic stranger who is pushing him away as hard as she can. Now, he's beginning to have real doubts about their future.

Sydney knows something's really wrong and she comes to my office to find out what to do. Clearly upset, she tells me she's tried being her normal self. But her usually accommodating manner is increasingly overrun by an engulfing rage that seems to erupt for no apparent reason. When I ask her if this behavior has occurred before, at first she says no but then remembers that the same inexplicable anger ended her first serious relationship with her college sweetheart.

"I was out of control then, and now I feel the same thing happening," she says, anxiously twisting her hands. "Why can't I just get a grip? I'm a basket case. What's the matter with me?"

Not only does Sydney feel completely miserable, but she also blames herself for not being able to control her actions. Sydney is convinced her emotional turmoil means there is something wrong with her. Like most people who walk through my door, she views being happy as a sort of report card: If she feels good, then she's doing life "right"; if she's in pain, then she's failing.

Sydney's pain is anything but failure, however. In fact, I tell her that it's the very thing that's going to free her from some very old, untrue messages she's been giving herself for years. These messages are part of an old story—one that has silently and invisibly instructed her for most of her life.

Sydney looks at me doubtfully when I tell her that the turmoil she's in is an important signal, and if she can just try to welcome it instead of pushing it away, it will be very useful to her. This doesn't make sense to her. Like most of us, she's been taught to avoid unpleasant feelings. Our culture is extremely pain averse, and we don't look at pain as a necessary part of life. There is no such thing as a deep emotional attachment in which we don't feel pain or anxiety at one point

10

or another. It's part of living. It's part of loving. Remove these emotions and you remove the intimacy. Yet we aren't raised to believe that living life fully means experiencing emotional messiness and anxiety and fear. We only see these feelings as something to be gotten rid of. Since we are never told about the value of pain, we, being human, simply look for ways to avoid or eliminate it.

Yet as we will see, difficult emotions enrich our lives in ways that we can't imagine. The path to getting what we want out of life runs right through all these messy, painful feelings. Trying to avoid them actually leads us astray. Feeling anger or rage or hate or frustration doesn't make us abnormal or sick or wrong or broken, it makes us *real*.

The Stories of Our Lives

We come into adulthood, like Sydney, believing certain things about ourselves. We recognize our characters, our behaviors, and ourselves. These are our personalities and identities. But what if I were to tell you that large parts of these personalities were based on fictions? You would dismiss me out of hand, probably. What a ridiculous notion! But take a look at the following list and ask yourself if you've ever experienced any of these things:

- You can't stop repeating behavior you absolutely don't want or intend.
- Your body breaks down or you often feel exhausted even when rested.
- Your anger becomes uncontrollable and larger than the situation warrants.

- You repeatedly date or marry the wrong person.
- You aren't happy with anything in your life and you feel unfulfilled.
- Your relationships have become embattled.
- You keep thinking that if you could just change something about yourself—make more money, lose weight, stop drinking—it would solve your problems.
- You believe that if you find that right someone, everything in your life will be complete.
- You believe that if you make a mistake, you will pay a steep price.
- You are always struggling against feeling down or empty even though on paper your life looks great.

All these—and more—are symptoms that you are living according to stories created so early in your life that you have no knowledge of them. You don't know they're calling the shots in your life and making you ill, dissatisfied, or prone to magical thinking. These fictions came out of a deep need that everyone has to stay attached to people they love even when those people hurt us, or disappointed us, put us down or abandoned us. These stories are the most human and natural things in the world. As children, we made them up to explain why the people we loved acted in ways that seemed painful to us. The stories made us feel safe even when the grown-ups in our lives didn't. They provided order; they kept us sane. They stopped us from being utterly over-whelmed by emotions and events in our lives. And the stories stay with us if they aren't exposed and updated. They don't change; they don't update. Sometimes they keep us feeling safe and loved, but more often, they start to break down in adulthood and cause us to act in the ways listed above. That's the one big problem with stories—they aren't real.

Sydney experienced quite a few of the symptoms listed above—out-of-character behavior, a repeated pattern, anger out of proportion to any situation—which told me she had a story that was breaking apart. In Sydney's case, most of her story was pretty unconscious. It didn't take long, though, for me to see what her story was. Deep inside, Sydney felt that she was insufficient as a woman. She was highly dependent emotionally on what she felt she could never have—the love of a man who would leave her because she wasn't "enough." This story created a whole personality: Sydney became a real people pleaser who excelled at figuring out what would make the people around her happy. She focused on satisfying their needs so they wouldn't look too deeply into hers. That skill became her principal connection to them. It also formed the core of her self-image, fueled her career, and was the currency of her relationships.

Yet when it counted most, her story backfired on her. Her compensatory personality (the one that instructed her not to show anyone how needy she was) allowed her to create only an incomplete relationship with Brian. She chose only selected parts of herself to show him. But she's done her job too well, and Brian's fallen in love with that person. He's gotten *too* close and now is in danger of seeing past her facade to her real shortcomings. Sydney's biggest unconscious fear is about to be realized: that a man will see how bad she is and then he'll leave her. Unconsciously, Sydney starts creating distance by freezing Brian out, picking on him, yelling at him for the slightest infraction. But her breakdown isn't working. Sydney's suffering a double loss at the moment: Not only is her fiancé about to take a walk but also her sense of self—the one the story created—is taking a real beating.

Sydney's completely unaware that all this is going on inside her.

Right now, she's just having a hard time seeing in her reflection the nice, generous, and care-taking person she always thought herself to be. What she sees is an angry, unpredictable, and moody woman. "Why would anyone want to be with such a shrew?" she asks. "I don't blame him one bit if he leaves. I am really horrible. I'm just as much a bitch as my mother."

Little does Sydney realize that she has just "outed" her story. It's taken getting to a place of tremendous fear and pain for her story to crumble and reveal the vulnerable child who created it in the first place. Sydney was eleven when her father left her mother for another woman. For several years before that, she got used to hearing her mother arguing with her father in the late evenings when they thought Sydney and her younger sister were sleeping. "No wonder he left," Sydney remembers thinking when she would see her mother's blotchy and swollen face in the morning.

Unconsciously, Sydney reacted to her father's abandonment by creating an explanation. Not only was her mother a screaming shrew (and thus, all women who yelled risked abandonment) but also Sydney herself was not lovable enough to hold on to him either. She was insufficient as a "woman" to keep her father at home. Too ugly. Too demanding. Too needy. Her new story told her that if she was going to avoid becoming her mother and having her mother's fate, she had to be an easy-going, submissive, and pleasing woman. It made sense when Sydney was a kid and well into her twenties. Indeed, the story served a good purpose for a very long time. It preserved her father as a good parent whose love she badly wanted. She needed to do that because he was gone. He was the absent parent. Sydney needed to hold on to his being a "good" parent who certainly would have loved her had she been good enough. Meanwhile, her mother had to accept the role of the witch in her daughter's mind because she stayed and was the present parent. Sydney could feel safe blaming her mother because her mother didn't abandon her.

This complex and inaccurate explanation placed the blame for her father's departure firmly on Sydney and her mother where, in her fantasies, she could have some control over it (after all, if she caused it, couldn't she cure it?). The story formed the foundation of her personality as a sensitive, accommodating woman. And it worked for a long time—until Brian came along. And then it didn't.

The Story's Cost

The old adage "Nothing in life is free" extends to the human psyche— Sydney has paid dearly for her fiction. It may have helped her avoid pain, but it also precluded any chance of real intimacy or real connection. How could she ever have the kind of give-and-take that is part of any good marriage? She couldn't. She would be too transparent. As long as her story tells her "you are not enough," her choices and her actions will be limited to those behaviors that distract everyone away from the insufficient woman she fears she is.

Sydney's story has robbed her of a relationship with her mother and left both women lonely and sad. Because she's blamed her mother for her father's departure all these years, she's been quick to dismiss her mother as a mean and bitter woman. Perhaps she is. But Sydney doesn't know that as a fact—she's never allowed herself to get close enough to find out. If she did and saw a loving and caring woman, the whole story on which she'd built her personality would crumble and Sydney couldn't take that risk.

Our stories cost us. They cost us in intimacy and in curiosity and in creativity. They demand that we stay within their safe boundaries—or else we will pay the ultimate price of rejection and abandonment. The stakes are always that high. We will see later on how essential these stories are to preserving our childhood selves, but if we don't break out of them in adulthood, they will constrict our choices and our lives.

Sydney's anguish leads her to the moment of choice—pay the price, lose Brian and keep the story, or lose the story and take the journey to becoming real.

Becoming Real

Becoming real begins when our stories start to collapse. When our orderly worlds become erratic, when we begin to see patterns of behavior we don't want in our lives, we are forced to see beyond the fiction. Becoming real isn't the same as being happy or free from pain. Becoming real is a wonderful state of richness and personal power that dwarfs anything else. Becoming real happens when we accept ourselves in our totality—the good, the bad, and the ugly, the strengths and the weaknesses. Becoming real doesn't happen overnight, nor is it possible without some effort, but when it happens, we experience a freedom unimagined. When we become real, we are able to have the exquisite connection to our lives and loved ones that can only come when we choose to stop pursuing the pain-avoidance filters that also keep out life's pleasure, meaning, and joy.

Yet, people come into my office every day wishing to feel better. They don't know that the real answer to their pain doesn't lie in being happy—that's not enough. We can be happy for a short period and change nothing. The answer to their desire is to listen to the painful feelings and have those emotions guide them to a richer, more wondrous place. But change is difficult and often doesn't feel good along the way. This is because real human connection involves pain. There is no way around it. Investing ourselves in our relationships means that at some point we will hurt. We will lose the affection of someone we love. We will disappoint and be disappointed. We will have conflict and betrayal. If we allow these fears to dominate us, we will keep our distance from close relationships or won't make intimate friends. We won't try to find mates—or we will, but we'll keep picking people with whom a relationship is destined to fail. We'll find ways to put distance between ourselves and our loved ones in order not to suffer. We'll find ourselves endlessly repeating unwanted behaviors that are the sources of the pain we feel.

The same holds true for our careers. If we are going to put ourselves out there and go for the satisfactions of true achievements, we are going to fail sometimes. We are not always going to live up to our potential; we are not always going to meet our expectations or those of others. There will sometimes be humiliation, frustration, and anger. There has to be. So if we are really, really terrified of feeling like failures, we'll pull back and not invest ourselves. We'll settle for that job that is less than we could achieve because it is a way of avoiding pain at all costs. But we will also have to forfeit the joy and confidence that come with having worked hard at something and having succeeded. We will have to live with that sinking sense of not ever having tested ourselves to see how much we could accomplish in our lives.

When we are real—and Sydney is going to have to become real if she wants a shot at that happiness she seeks—we start to see that ambivalent feelings are natural, normal, and unavoidable parts of life. We understand that loving means risking being hurt, disappointed, or angry. If Sydney is willing to change her goal from "feeling better" to understanding what lies beneath these huge feelings, she's going to get the ultimate payoff—she'll get the great satisfaction and power of being who she really is instead of who she fears she isn't. Being truly real doesn't mean she won't have pain or conflict in her marriage, but it does mean she will have the power to make decisions about how she'll respond to these feelings and not be ruled by them. She'll stop flying off the handle at the slightest provocation, and she won't have to live her life terrified of being left.

The only way for Sydney to enjoy this powerful way of living—the only way for all of us—is not to turn away from painful or negative emotions but to embrace them and understand them. They lead to the unconscious mind and to the stories it creates that keep us from being real. It is only by understanding the unconscious—that fantastic spinner of tales—that we are able to make the deep and meaningful changes that result in rich, real lives.

The Unconscious

We are not a simple species with simple reactions to external stimuli. We don't have set responses to other people, places, or events in our lives. Our minds are like pearls with each layer building on the one laid down before it until the way we respond to our lives rests on all the combined previous experiences. We all have genetic wiring that determines to varying degrees how we will respond to losses, disappointments, abandonments, or betrayals. But we also have a complex mechanism—the unconscious—that absorbs our experiences and searches for its own way to make sense of what happens to us. In other words, it creates a narrative to bring order to and explain our experiences.

Simply put, the unconscious is all the thoughts that are not in our awareness. Our lives are powerfully guided by it in fundamental ways. It's involuntary—much like breathing or a beating heart. The unconscious is like a black box: experiences go into it, and almost automatically out comes an explanation about what has happened to us and how we should react to it. The unconscious issues its own instructions on how to act and react to the people and events in our lives. It is a source of profound energy and creativity, but the stories it creates operate according to an interior and invisible set of rules and logic that almost never corresponds to what is actually happening around us. The unconscious does not differentiate between what happened twenty minutes ago and what happened twenty years ago. That's how Sydney can blow up over nothing: Her unconscious story tells her she's about to be abandoned, and that makes her enraged. But she's reacting to something that isn't real.

What we need to do is learn how to recognize when our unconscious mind has created stories that still whisper things in our ears. They can be simple things—like never owning anything with stripes because you believe you look fat in them—to more complex instructions like the time Sydney (who was terrified of heights) went flying with Brian because she was afraid if she didn't he'd leave her. This book will show you how to expose these fantasies' messages so that we, not the unconscious, can control our lives.

The unconscious expresses itself through our stories (I will also refer to them as fantasies or myths). The story is the fundamental message we tell ourselves about ourselves—a message we don't consciously choose. It instructs us about who we are and who we aren't, what is safe and what is perilous. It gives us its version of how events and interactions in our lives are "destined" to turn out. It speaks to us most often about our fears or perceived inadequacies. These unconscious stories operate below our radars, yet our personalities and our lives are infused with their messages. When we are unaware of the unconscious and its stories, it can direct our choices and cause all sorts of problems and pain. We can become self-destructive by alienating friends, bucking authority at work, or bingeing on food or alcohol. We can lose control by yelling at our children, not sticking up for ourselves, or repeating unwanted behaviors like promiscuous sex or reckless driving. We smoke too much, argue too much. We find ways to hedge our bets or screw up our emotional commitments. It helps us pick the wrong boyfriend or girlfriend. We do exactly what we know will get us in trouble with the boss. Yet we can't seem to help ourselves. The stories from our unconscious can rule us with their impulses—causing the very situations and feelings we were hoping to avoid.

It's Sydney's unconscious conflict between wanting love and fearing its loss that's kicking up and causing such problems in her life. Deep within, her unconscious story automatically makes her respond to a fear that in reality has nothing to do with Brian. It's causing her to reject his tenderness while demanding his attention. It's making her lose her sex drive while waking in the middle of the night in a cold sweat that he'll leave her. Her unconscious story recycles old fears and failures and sends her messages that make her behave irrationally and in uncharacteristic ways and cause her to feel she's "not acting like herself."

The Stories That Keep Us from Being Real

The trickiest part of the unconscious story is that it is a fantasy that masquerades as reality. It may look and feel and taste like the truth to us; it may feel familiar and right. That makes sense because our stories have been with us for a long time. They color how we see everything, but we don't know we are looking at the world through the distorting prism of the story—it looks like reality to us. Therefore, it makes sense to resist examining our stories because they are such a deep and integral part of who we are, even if they're standing between us and a deeper, richer life experience. It gets a little easier to motivate ourselves when we can see them as the fertile ground for our anxieties, compulsions, and problematic patterns of behavior. But if you find yourself bridling at the suggestion of even having a story, realize that your reaction is completely sensible—who wouldn't resist risking what we think makes us safe?

Most stories are created in response to the deep emotional fears of rejection or abandonment or the actual experience of them. They provide explanations for the incomprehensible or overwhelmingly painful events in our lives. We have a story about our personalities, our abilities, our families, our strengths, and our weaknesses. In fact, much of our personalities are based on our stories. At one point in our lives—usually early on—these stories served a purpose for us. They helped us explain why something painful that was out of our control like the death of a parent or a separation from divorce or even the birth of a sibling happened at all.

As we mature, these childhood explanations serve as the foundation for much of who we become—but the only problem is, these stories are distorted and incomplete. A woman whose mother had cancer when she was in her womb and died shortly after her birth grows up with the unconscious story that she will be harmful to anyone who gets close. Not surprisingly, although she says she wants a family of her own, she's only dated unavailable men her whole life, and now, at forty-two, realizes that it's not just bad luck that she didn't get married; it's the fantasies from the story that are undermining her. A man whose mother never held him and constantly criticized him grew up to become a beloved pediatrician so he could give what he never got. But his story tells him he never was worthy so he never feels he has succeeded. The story constellations are endless.

Why don't we spot these stories when they start operating in our lives? Why does it take so many failed relationships, blown opportunities, and so much misery before we see them? Because stories work! Sometimes, they keep us safe for a long time. They shield us from things that hurt too much to bear; they create emotional comfort where there is none. There are a million and one things that can set up these unconscious stories—anything from the death of a beloved pet to the arrival of a sibling. None of us gets through childhood without developing one. It's important to understand that stories are not "bad" or pathological or unbalanced. They're human nature. We respond to losses and traumatic events by creating a narrative that helps us make sense of what's happened.

Not every story is created as a defense. Many stories just are. In fact, sometimes stories can be "good," serving us well and improving our emotional well-being. There is a part of our minds that is in our awareness, and there is a part that isn't. From a purely Darwinian approach, you could certainly say that some experiences are too painful and need to be processed a little at a time. Having a place to be out of your awareness is a good thing. If after 9/11 everybody was walking around thinking that at any second a bomb could destroy them, how could anyone function? We have to know a little about what is going on to protect ourselves, but we also have to be able to tuck the powerful fears away somewhere so we can keep going to work and raising our families and doing all the stuff that we do.

Not every story comes out of traumatic experiences or big losses. Our stories exist as natural repositories for our emotional experiences. We have to share our parents with our siblings, and we have to explain to ourselves why we are not the sole focus of their attentions. We may "hate" our best friends if we lose a competition to them, and then if something bad happens to them, we may blame ourselves because we think our bad feelings magically caused the problems. Or we may get dumped in a particularly mean way by our first love. The unconscious tries to make sense of these things. It experiences the loss and fear, and it reacts in kind. Much of how we respond to our lives depends on our innate natures. Some of us are born with more aggression, more anxiety, more sexual drive, or more intensity than others. An event like a divorced parent's remarriage can be more traumatic for an innately competitive person than for a more easy-going person. A story is neither good nor bad—it just is. Its purpose is to help us explain and resolve the emotional conflicts we experience as children. But as we will see, unless we become aware of these stories as we grow older, these child-based stories can cause all sorts of adult conflicts; therefore, we must expose them, rewrite them, and overcome them.

These stories will be the central focus of this book, because in order to become real, we must learn to spot when they're directing our lives and become willing to move beyond them. You will see that the stories have common themes that create five distinct personality types depending on when in our lives the stories begin. People who feel worthless work overtime to become tremendously successful yet never feel so. Others who feel they are unlovable compensate by bending over backward to stay connected to loved ones. It takes a lot of work and effort to keep up with our stories' demands. It's hard to get joy out of our achievements because they are powered by fictitious beliefs served up by the unconscious. That's the sad part about all this. People walk around saying, "I have achieved X, Y, and Z, so why am I not happy? Why am I so scared all the time or depressed and feeling that it's all just not enough?" When achievement compensates for an inner lacking, it does not fix the feelings that we are not lovable. We still teeter on the edge of being rejected or abandoned all the time.

Our stories may propel us forward, but only by rear-wheel drive. When that happens, fear is pushing us to act. We need to ask ourselves, Is this the way we want to live our lives? What is the measure of a good life—external rewards or a sense of internal integrity? If we are fearful and dissatisfied even as we excel, if we are driven forward by feelings of worthlessness, will we ever be able to appreciate our accomplishments, or will we simply sit there and add one more notch in our belt?

The good news is that, no matter what created our stories, we all have a chance to move beyond them. This opportunity comes when our stories stop protecting us, and begin interfering in our lives by causing pain, disruption, and all sorts of emotional chaos. When our lives stop functioning, as awful as those moments may be, we become willing to dig deeply into the unconscious and see what's causing all the problems. Until we explore the negative feelings, until we take our fantasies out into the open and look at them, they will have the upper hand.

My hope for people who use this book is that they will gain that personal freedom and strength that being real brings—that they won't have to be as afraid of bad things happening in life. If we are real, we become sturdy, and we will have the ability to surmount life's natural difficulties.

Nothing but exposing our stories as fantasies will help us in becoming real. Nothing else will sustain us through a lifetime of what we want to do. We don't want to put a bandage on our pain that will fall off when the realities of life come along—when we don't get the promotion we hoped for or our children fall ill or our parents age and die. When we are real, we can deal with those painful passages that are just a part of life.

Once we understand our unconscious stories, we will be able to see past them and embrace lives that are interesting and intricate and rich. I think to actually experience that joy, we must go through the process of exposing and exploding our fantasies. This process of becoming real is about maturity. It is also about living without a fog around you.

For the purpose of moving forward in our lives, we need to understand where our stories came from and how we came up with them, and to hold them up to the light of our present days. We need to see how our fantasies get in the way of our realities. They stop us because we get stuck in them. When we are stuck in the "If I'm a normal good girl then I'll feel complete when I am walking down the aisle" story, then we can't admit to being ambivalent about getting married. Yet our ultimate happiness may depend completely on a careful examination of what is making us of two minds. When we explore and then explode our personal myths, we can think through what we're going to do. As painful as it might be to see that we are marrying the wrong person, it's a whole lot better than actually marrying him or her.

In the next few chapters, I will share with you the process that will help you reach past your defenses into your unconscious. It begins with reading stories—because the more you see other people's stories, the easier it is to spot one of your own. I will show you how the unconscious mind resists discovery with a complex but very identifiable set of defenses. There will be moments in your exploration when you are filled with denial or anxiety. Please know that these are natural and indeed are excellent signs that you are on the right track. While we all may have unique stories, the process outlined here—that of seeing your story, seeing your defenses, tracing its roots, and becoming aware of how this story has governed your behavior—is the same for everyone. I cannot guarantee what you will find, but I can tell you that you will discover you've been living in two dimensions in a three-dimensional world. You will have the experience of being authentic, strong, rooted. You will be able to withstand the pain of loss and feel the joy of closeness, connection, intimacy. Being real means experiencing the full spectrum of human emotions instead of living a dampened-down and numb existence. You will have the strength, the stamina, the courage, the power, and the freedom to guide yourself to where you want to go.

Chapter Two

THE PRIMARY
EMOTIONAL STORIES

The easiest way to understand where our stories come from is to see them as something we create that allows us to satisfy our deepest and most basic needs. All people are born with both innate temperaments and these natural instinctual needs. Some of us are born active, some passive, some aggressive, some shy. Some of us need a lot of attention; others are very self-sufficient. But we all need to love and be loved. We need to be able to become distinct individuals and to be able to express ourselves as such. We are like rivers—when any one of these drives is blocked or frustrated, we don't stop flowing, we just find another less direct route to what we need. Since what we all need is love and connection, we bend and twist into any shape necessary that allows us to hold on to that love's source. No one is born a natural doormat, yet many stories teach us to lie down and accept any behavior to sustain our relationships. And over time, we accept the stories as gospel.

Once Upon a Time

Our stories start with our hardwiring. Each of us is born a unique being. Many of us have had the experience of looking at our children and marveling how one came out of the womb easygoing and cheery while another has an intensity almost absent in her sibling. We look at our own sisters and brothers and wonder, "How could we be from the same family?" We all have our own mental hardwiring that allows us to process the same information differently.

But that hardwiring only takes us so far. The real development of our characters, or our personalities (and I use those words more or less interchangeably), begins when that innate wiring connects with an environment. As infants, our caregivers and families comprise that world. From our earliest moments, our interactions with them determine what kinds of people we will become and what kind of stories we will tell ourselves about our characters and our lives.

Since we all need love and security, whatever is going on in our environments will either meet our emotional needs or it won't. When we are unsatisfied, or feel ignored, unconsciously, we instinctually start scrambling. We immediately need to (1) find a new way of connecting and (2) absolve the loved one from any responsibility for the dissatisfaction because we still need them to care for us, and, without that protection, we'll die. No one consciously does this. It's automatic and happens outside of our awareness. Creating a story is a survival skill, a coping mechanism, and an ordering principle. Without our stories to keep us tied to the people we need, tremendous anxiety would occur. As children, we need these fantasies to feel safe and loved and accepted, but as grown-ups, they can get in our way.

I can't emphasize enough that *how* we fit into our surroundings can be as important as whether our parents did or didn't respond appropriately to our needs. Not having our needs met does not mean we have to start parent-bashing. Certainly, how our parents interacted with us does makes a huge difference in how our personalities develop. But how we match up to our surroundings also determines our lives.

Ada's mother had a physical syndrome that caused extreme sensitivity to anything loud or bright. Hearing thumps and shrieks gave her intense headaches. Her first child was a docile boy who cried as all babies do, but most of the time he was happy to sit and coo and play by himself. Ada, however, was her brother's opposite. She developed colic and spent the first three months of her life bawling her head off. "My mother used to say I came out screaming and never stopped," she told me. Ada came to my office as an adult with chronic colitis. Her story told her that no one would love her if she complained, so she let her colitis symptoms get so out of hand that she nearly died. It took being hospitalized for Ada to see that she was taking instructions from a very old story. Her mother, now dead, would have been stunned to hear how her inadvertent message had mutated over the years. Ada's mother loved her dearly, as dearly as she loved Ada's brother. But she couldn't soothe her and carry her around as she needed to without tremendous physical pain. This was a mismatch of needs about which nothing could be done. It happens all the time.

Jonathan grew up in a strictly orthodox Jewish family. He spent much of his life separated from women and thus was completely unprepared for his role as father of a zesty, developing teenage girl. Her innate and healthy sexuality overwhelmed him, and he had no knowledge of or experience in how to deal with a normal teen with raging hormones. His only response involved disappearing into his study whenever she was around. This girl adored her father and needed his love. She needed an explanation for his rejection of her, and since it coincided with her budding womanhood, she created a story that told her to hide her sexuality since it meant people would abandon her. This girl's need to be recognized and accepted was overpowered by her need to love her father. She made herself "wrong" in order to make him "right." She preserved him as a "good" father and made the problem her budding sexuality. He meant her no harm. He loved his daughter but was just not able to deal with her femininity.

I can give innumerable examples of parents who truly adore their children but who, for their own involuntary reasons, were unable to respond adequately to their kids' needs at important developmental times. Some were distant; others too close. Some weren't tolerant; others too liberal. We aren't given a choice about who we are and who our children are. Sometimes the match is a good one, and sometimes it isn't.

When the match isn't good, we experience a conflict between our basic drives or needs and our environment's ability to fulfill them. That's where the stories come in—we can't get rid of the drives and don't want to get rid of the loved ones, so we find a way to explain the frustration we experience when we are unfulfilled or misunderstood.

Also key to our character development is *when* things happen in our lives. When a big emotional event—it can be traumatic or just highly charged—coincides with one of our developmental stages, it affects our stories and our personalities. Some kids can have a sibling fall ill and be fine. For others, it can change their whole approach to intimacy. For instance, one of my patients was four years old when her one-and-a-half-year-old brother came down with meningitis. She had been experiencing an increase of the sibling rivalry/competitive feelings phase where she had wished her brother had never been born. When he almost died, my patient became wracked with guilt and haunted by the sense that she possessed a kind of magical evil power that caused her brother harm. She has carried this fear with her through her relationships ever since. It is now integrated into her character, and her story has become that people she loves intensely could come to harm, particularly if she gets angry with them. This is not about her innate wiring, a conflict, an instinctual drive, or how she fits into her family. Because it happened at a developmentally vulnerable stage, it affected the development of her personality. If it had happened at another time, it might not have been an issue at all.

Sometimes a story has its origins in a random incident. When Penny was six or seven—she doesn't remember which—she ran into her parents' bathroom to get something. There, standing behind the glass shower door, was her father. He didn't see Penny but she saw him. He was fully erect, washing himself. Penny had never seen a man's penis before but was at an age where she knew what one was and vaguely understood its function. Penny stood riveted to the spot. She couldn't take her eyes off her father and felt both excitement and horror at the same time. In a split second, Penny's paradoxical feelings about sex originated. Penny developed a story that she was a "bad" girl to feel excited—a perfectly age-appropriate response. Thirty years later, the story still held its power. Penny came to see me because she'd become so conflicted about her sexual drive that she no longer functioned with her husband when they were making love. We begin to see how potent stories are when we realize that what happens in a split second can cast a shadow over many years.

We can't choose between our hardwiring or our caregivers—we need both. So we create stories that explain why something happened or why we didn't get what we needed in ways that allow us to stay connected to the people we love because, after all, we still need them. Because this happens so early in life, the story we create becomes the primer coat for everything else we are going to experience in the future.

The Primary Colors of Emotional Needs

It turns out that in our development as people, timing is everything. Disappointments and frustrations that we absorb handily at one age can deck us at another. Each story is born when we don't have an emotional need fulfilled or when a natural expression of who we are gets frustrated. We are all born with certain urges that must be attended to. I like to think of these as the primary colors of emotional needs. If we peel away all the layers of experience in our lives, at the core we will find the same four needs:

- The need to attach
- The need to be allowed to become individuals
- The need to express ourselves
- The need to be seen for who we are with acceptance (also known as attunement)

These colors may present themselves in countless shades, but if we trace them back far enough, following them through the twists and turns of what has happened to us, we eventually arrive at these four primary needs. These needs never go away. What we do to have them fulfilled becomes the story that will inform the rest of our lives.

Attachment

Alan's father was an alcoholic and behaved very erratically. When he was sober, he adored Alan. He would spend time pushing him in his carriage and, when Alan got a little older, teaching him how to throw a baseball. But when he had too much to drink, he often humiliated Alan publicly for the slightest infraction. Each time this happened, it would terrify Alan—he was so afraid of being left alone. While others could see that Alan's father had real problems and was neither a successful man nor a very good role model, Alan was unable to look at his father that way. He needed a man he could love, admire, and depend on. So he created a story that idealized his father, turning him into someone worth holding on to. Alan re-created his father as strong, individualistic, and spontaneous instead of unpredictable and volatile. This fiction explained the unpredictability. But, most important, it created a worthy father, someone who could be depended on.

Alan's story comes out of the first need we all experience—the need to attach and bond to a loved one. In Alan's case, because he needed his father to survive physically and emotionally, he had to create a fiction that resolved and explained the conflict between the inadequate father who existed and the adequate father Alan needed.

This first emotional need obviously has biological significance. As helpless infants, we must be attached to someone who will sacrifice for us, feed us, and keep us alive, since we are unable to do all of this for ourselves. Attachment is a purely instinctual drive but not a simple one. Studies have shown that, immediately after birth, infants do what they can to interact with those around them. By three months, infants even respond to a parent's emotional state. If a parent looks upset or happy, infants react by getting upset or happy.

This need to stay attached to our loved ones is so powerful, so primal, that it affects our relationships with people for the rest of our lives. Alan had learned at such an early age not to trust his source of affection that, as an adult, he had tremendous difficulties whenever he got into an intimate relationship. He'd start out great but then find himself feeling inadequate around the woman he loved and would become increasingly distant and overly apologetic about everything, driving the woman nuts. Consequently, as desperately as he wanted to get married and have a family, at fifty-two it looked like he was going to be a lifelong bachelor.

When we get the opportunity to fully attach to our loved ones, later in life our stories won't send us messages that we are awful people and have to hide our true needs and natures from people we love. I had a patient whose mother died in a car accident shortly after she was born. Many different family members took turns caring for her while she was an infant until an aunt stepped in to care for her permanently when she turned two. My patient experienced this period of upheaval as a chain of multiple abandonments. Ultimately, she became extremely adept at suppressing any needs she had for fear that if she needed something or someone, they would experience her needs as a burden and leave her. My patient's story instructed her to become highly independent and appear virtually need-free. But that didn't make the need itself go away. Inside, she was also very afraid that if anyone saw how truly needy she was for love and attention, they would run for the hills. Her sister had been ten when their mother died and didn't experience these abandonments the same way because she was at a different stage in her life—one not as developmentally vulnerable to this kind of trauma. She experienced none of her sister's kinds of problems.

Because our need to attach is so primary and starts so early, whatever story we create about any disruption (and we all have them) echoes down the corridors of our lives. But it's a bit like the game of telephone. As the story gets farther and farther from its original source, it morphs into something that is often quite unrecognizable. It takes sleuthing to follow the story's clues back to their source. When we can do that, we can switch from an old and infantile solution to a mature, adult one. We switch from fantasy to reality. This is also true for the following three needs.

Individuation

Lilly's mother was a woman who just wasn't able to deal with controversy. This was too bad, because Lilly liked to debate. It was just in Lilly's nature to push back at everyone. But because Lilly's mother had her own issues with conflict from her own childhood, every time Lilly would contradict her mom or express a different opinion, her mother would come down on her like a ton of bricks. Each time this happened, Lilly felt the devastation of complete rejection. Not surprisingly, Lilly learned how to do a couple of things—push away any anger she started to feel (because if she wasn't angry then her mother would love her) and express the anger she did have (because we all have anger) extremely indirectly. Many years later, Lilly arrived in my office with an ulcer, an excessively cheery personality (that drove everyone around her nuts), and a marriage that was on the rocks because her husband couldn't take her passive aggression anymore.

Lilly's mother frustrated her need to be an individual with her own opinions. But the way the mind works, in order to hold on to a loving and lovable mother, Lilly blocked the expression of her own needs. She did that for the same reason we all do—because it allows us to stop doing the thing that keeps causing the terrible pain—in Lilly's case, being rejected by her mother. It also allows us to preserve the love object that we need so desperately.

We all need to become individuals, and we do this by exploring the world on our own. This creates a separation between us and our loved ones that can cause all sorts of anxiety and disruption if we don't feel safe going off on our own. During this phase of our development, we begin to create boundaries—not just physical separations but mental and emotional ones, too. We first realize that we have an independent ability to think something that someone else isn't thinking of. As soon as we start to separate from our parents and loved ones, we begin our lives as separate individuals.

We start to feel a sense of autonomous power for the first time. We see that we can affect our own body functions and impact our environments to some degree. That's important because this is when we learn to express anger. As we start individuating, we realize for the first time that we can control our own emotions. We start wondering how much power we have to be different and affect our environments according to our desires. "If I get angry, what will it do?" we wonder. "Can I use my anger to control others?"

When our individuality gets thwarted at this stage, we create stories in which people can't express emotions directly without causing themselves pain. When Sam was five, every time he got angry, his father completely blew a gasket. "That is completely unacceptable! How dare you oppose me?" he would thunder and slam out of the room, leaving Sam alone to face his misdeed. All by himself, Sam would panic—and become enraged at being left behind. Sam began to equate his rage with his father's abandonment, so he learned to stop his feelings one step ahead of their expression. When the anger started to well up, he would say to himself (not in these exact words, but in the language of the unconscious), "You are a bad person if you ever get angry." By doing this, Sam believed he'd found a way to keep his father while preserving the image of his dad as a good guy. Rather than saying to himself, "Wow, Dad is a horrible asshole," Sam elevated his father while blaming himself.

Sam's story became "I have to let other people rule me so that they'll love me and not leave me. I can't be angry with anyone because I will be left alone and angry." This kind of story keeps people from being real because they develop a false self. Their real selves (and every person has one) are pissed off, because there's not a person on earth who doesn't get angry.

All kids need to manage their own anger—and parents are charged with showing them how. The goal is to have children be aware of and express their anger without being overwhelmed by it in an out-of-control rage. But when their primary need to express themselves is obliterated by a parent's inability to tolerate any anger at all, then something else is happening. It's an unfair fight. We want kids to be able to manage conflicts—after all, our lives are made up of them. Unfortunately, in pop psychology, people have come to think of conflict as "bad," but this is not necessarily so. Conflict is nothing but two opposing ideas. We need conflicts—they keep us socialized. They keep us from overstepping our boundaries. But when we are trying to understand where our stories and our personalities come from, we must see the difference between having different views and a conflict between a basic need and a source of love. These are the conflicts that create stories.

Expression

Sandy's father left his mother when he was eight. The middle child of three children and the only boy, it was Sandy to whom his mother turned when she was down. She depended on him to help her keep the house running, and consequently he grew up quickly. But when, as a teenager, Sandy expressed interest in girls, his mother became quite jealous of and derogatory toward any girls he was interested in. She began to act cold and distant whenever Sandy disobeyed her or went out on a date. When he announced he wanted to be a rock musician and started a rock band, she didn't talk to him for three days. Her disapproval permeated everything, leaving Sandy feeling horribly guilty every time he felt the stirrings of his natural inclinations.

Ultimately, Sandy caved in to his mother's pressure. At college, instead of being a music major, he declared pre-med. All his life he'd heard her say that he should become a doctor like her father. When Sandy ultimately went to medical school and became an orthopedic surgeon, it proved to her that she hadn't been such a bad mother under the circumstances and that all Sandy's early responsibility paid off in the end.

On Sandy's fortieth birthday, his world started to crumble. His story that had followed him out of his childhood was that, to be a good guy and be loved by his mother and therefore feel secure, he had to be a good doctor, husband, son, and father. But his story also carried the darker side of his father's example. He'd been the one with all the freedom. When he walked out on Sandy, his mother, and his sisters, he'd set the example of what a real man looked like—a rebel, a man above commitment, a free spirit. As much as Sandy resented his father, he loved him even more, and Sandy was conflicted between being the man who earned his mother's love and approval and wanting to be a man like his father.

Because of this conflict and in spite of the fact that he loved his wife and kids, Sandy had begun acting out with other women. The chief of surgery reprimanded him for his increasingly strident attitude. Sandy, having been obedient for so long, started to blow up his life bit by bit. Because his need for expression had been blocked at a critical stage, he'd grown up acting out his mother's drama. Now, he had nowhere to turn but to the fantasy of what a man should be. The myth of his father battled with his frustrations caused by his mother. A powerful conflict resulted. When this basic need is frustrated, it goes underground and creates tremendous havoc down the road.

As we get older, we need to be able to express our budding unique selves. This drive comes in as we explore how we will fit into the world. It is through the need for expression that we match up our dreams, ambitions, and ideals with our abilities. This requires gauging the difference between what we can attempt and what our actual abilities are. When we try for too much or reach for more than we can handle, this drive either becomes frustrated or we begin to feel inadequate.

When self-expression is blocked, we learn to pretend (to ourselves and to others) to be somebody else. Seeking approval, we migrate from who we really are to who we think our parents or teachers or grandparents want us to be. We adopt their expectations for who we should be, and we learn to value someone else's opinion of who we are more than our own fragile and inadequate selves.

This story creates personalities that often act out self-destructively, as Sandy did. Just because the ability to express our true nature gets blocked, it doesn't mean the need to express ourselves goes away. But it gets twisted and conflicted. Our authentic drives cry to be let out but our stories pen them in and disrespect them.

Attunement

The last drive is the need for attuned love relationships. By attuned I don't mean just feeling bonded to people and having them take care of our most basic needs. An attuned relationship is one in which we feel fully seen and understood. We all need to feel "I get you, you get me" and to feel that we have an impact on and are impacted on by the world around us. Also in this stage falls one of the key factors in our development. This is where our parents' (and others') abilities—or lack thereof—to deal with our natural sexuality, aggression, and competition make their mark on our personalities. Inappropriate responses at this stage create all sorts of problems.

When Nancy's father bought her a slinky nightgown for her fifteenth birthday, her mother was horrified. "Oh, it's what all the girls are wearing," he told her with a laugh. "Get with it." Nancy, too, felt uncomfortable with the gift, but she rationalized her feelings by saying she was pretty sure her father didn't mean anything by it. But he did always have a comment about how good she looked, how he bet the boys would love her tank top, and how, if he were a boy, he'd be all over her. Nancy started to feel very ashamed of her body and of her femininity. Ten years later, Nancy came to me worried that she had no sexual drive. "If I hear from one more man that I'm a tease, I will freak," she said. It seems that Nancy, who had a knockout figure and liked to show it off, didn't really enjoy sex all that much. Her boyfriends often became angry because of the inconsistency between her come-ons and follow-throughs.

A story doesn't have to be complicated to be powerful. Nancy's father's inappropriate sexual comments—and their consequently unattuned relationship—certainly created a split inside Nancy. As she grew older, the emotional need to stay attached to her father naturally migrated into a need to have a relationship with a man. But the terms under which that relationship operated also stayed the same—for her father, she felt she had to be sexy to hold his love and gain his approval even at the cost of her own sense of comfort and appropriateness. Now, as an adult, the same rules unconsciously dictated how she was going to behave with other men—hence her sexy demeanor wrapped around a hollow and conflicted inside.

When we aren't recognized for who we are in our entirety, it throws everything out of proportion. As Nancy did, we end up emphasizing one part of our characters—our sexuality, our brains, our talent—so much that it overshadows our other gifts. Our personalities become stretched out of shape, and we become dogged by feelings of shame, low self-esteem, and a sense of being an imposter.

How the Primary Emotions Create a Story

Each of these primary emotional needs has a sequence, and there are natural frustrations that happen at each stage. How those needs are either met or frustrated creates our stories and ultimately our personalities. What do I mean by "frustration"? I don't mean the feeling that we call frustration as in "I get so frustrated in traffic" or "My boss is so frustrating." What I mean here is something much more powerful. When any or all of the four primary needs gets frustrated, what do we experience? Rage, terror, grief. We're too young to have a moderated emotional response. We experience any frustration, abandonment, rejection, or abuse—no matter the degree—at a survival level, and that inspires big emotional responses.

So what do we do? First and foremost, to survive, we have to find a way to stay attached to the very people who have disappointed or hurt us. We can't allow them to be at fault—we need them to be strong and dependable for our survival. So, if they can't be to blame, then we erroneously conclude that the problem must lie with us. All this happens silently, totally outside of our awareness. But if these fearful conclusions could be put into words, they would sound a lot like this:

- I am broken and will be abandoned.
- I am inadequate and unlovable.
- Life is not fair and I will be denied the love I seek.

These painful conclusions become our starting points as we twist our realities, re-creating them as the stories we tell ourselves to explain why our needs haven't been met.

Any number of events can trigger our stories' creation—the birth of a sibling, the illness of a grandparent, even stern responses to childish behavior. Anything that separates us from our caregivers is enough to put us in a heightened state of red alert. Since we are just too young and powerless to do anything about the state of the world around us, we bend ourselves in ways we think will keep us attached—we learn to become silent when we're needy or coquettish when we're ignored, or to hurt ourselves when we're angry at others. We will see that these very crude but effective solutions to our perceived problems ultimately determine our personalities.

When we get older and are denied attention or affection, we have better coping skills to help us understand and weather the power of these feelings. We have perspective and tools and sources outside our immediate family that provide us with feedback and reality checks. But as children, these feelings and the fears they evoke overwhelm us and create unbearable anxiety. Our unconscious comes to the rescue by creating a story about what's going on.

Rather than continuing to feel the bad feelings that come out of the disappointments, rejections, and feelings of being ignored or belittled, stories create a way for us to take control of our lives. We take these frustrations inside and explain their existence in a way that denies our own needs.

And so our personalities begin.

Let's go back to Sam for a moment. Rather than live with the terror of his father's retaliatory rage, Sam learned to block his own feelings of anger. He even learned to deny that they existed. But as an adult, a pattern started showing up in Sam's life. A girlfriend he loved broke off their relationship because she couldn't stand how his passive-aggressive behavior always brought out her nasty side. At work, the more subservient he became, the angrier his boss got. Ultimately, he fired Sam. No one wanted to be near him since he brought out the worst in people. Sam's story, "I have to be a doormat to make people like me," worked with his father but not with the mature world. His girlfriend and boss wanted to deal with Sam, not with the character created by his story.

Sam's story (which he created as his solution for keeping his father's love) ended up as the cornerstone of his personality. This is true for us all—the stories we tell ourselves about why our primary needs aren't being satisfied determine a great deal of who we become. Sure, some of that character is hardwired, but the rest is formed by our response to the frustration. No child can withstand the pain caused by the fear of abandonment. But the alternative is equally untenable—children cannot risk seeing their loved ones as unlovable people because that, too, amounts to a separation and abandonment.

When this happens, we do the only thing we can—we broker a peace at our own expense. By making ourselves "inadequate" or "bad," by dismissing our needs and desires as "wrong" or "excessive," we get to hold on to the ideal parents we all want and need emotionally. *We turn ourselves into pretzels to avoid pain and maintain love.* It's completely understandable. We twist more and more away from our "real" selves because this contortion allows us to avoid deep pain. Each time it works, we are willing to do it again and again and again. That's why it's so hard to change a self-destructive habit. We created the behavior so early and with such good reasons that giving up our accustomed coping mechanisms recalls the feelings of the immediate dangers of those long-ago feared rejections—rejections we had to avoid in order to live. Thus, through our stories, we found a way to avoid frustration, pain, and anxiety. Each time we repeat our stories to ourselves ("It's not a good idea to defy or get angry . . ."), we become more and more comfortable with our solutions. They become part of how we respond to the world and literally become "second" nature.

All this translates into a tremendous loss—the loss of an authentic self, one capable of authentic relationships. A woman who, like Sam, had a very easily threatened and therefore intolerant parent—in her case, it was her mother—developed the story that if she said yes to everyone, then they would love her. By the time I met her, you could almost see the anger coming out of her pores. Her story may have allowed her to have held on to the connection to her mother as a kid, but now she finds herself unable to turn to her husband and say, "I'm sick of making dinner every night!" For her, this wouldn't be expressing a completely acceptable irritation; it would be equal to risking total rejection and abandonment. She maintained her love at too high a price. The price was loss of peace of mind and absolutely no intimacy with her husband. When we can't acknowledge anger or disappointment, we also rob ourselves of the ability to forgive. Forgiving those we love—our parents, our spouses, our children—is necessary for real intimacy and contentment in a close relationship. Making peace with the things you don't like in your loved ones allows you to love them more fully.

Chapter Three

HOW STORIES KEEP US FROM OUR TRUE SELVES

I can't depend on anyone but myself."

"If only I were thinner, richer, more successful, or prettier, I would be happy."

"There's a right way and a wrong way to do everything, and his way is wrong."

"I can't do anything wrong or I'll pay."

"When I'm married (or married to the right person), I'll be happy."

"I'm too needy."

"I can't take it when someone gets mad at me."

"If I'm not number one, then why bother?"

"My problems are all my parents' (or spouse's or boss's) fault."

"People don't give me the credit I deserve."

"If I let them win, they'll like me."

When I hear statements like these—and I do every day in my office—I know I'm listening to someone's story. Conclusions like these look simple enough on the surface. They sound like reasonable truths based on experience. However, they are not based in reality at all but on fictions made up long ago that explained why we felt unlovable or inadequate or wrong. I think of these story themes as humanity's "greatest hits" because most of us know how to hum at least one of them.

As I mentioned in the last chapter, everyone has a story, and most of us have more than one. They are the threads that weave the fabric of our personalities. They may even make us interesting and textured and colorful. Having stories is the most natural thing in the world, and we couldn't get rid of them even if we wanted to. As we saw in the last chapter, they are born of great pain and fear and come from our most tender and vulnerable places. We needed them to make sense of our world and to survive the unavoidable emotional upheavals of early development.

But what happens as we get older? Remember that stories are the products of our unconscious minds—we aren't even aware of their existence. Because we can't tell if they are operating in our lives, we aren't able to bring them out periodically and update them as we change and grow as we do with our clothes, our hairstyles, and even our friends. Instead, the reliable fictions sit like silent navigators directing us back to the familiar crude and primal solutions of our early childhoods. Well into adulthood they tell us, "Hold on to love. Trade who you are for what you think is a more acceptable version of yourself—the one without the neediness, the demands, the imperfections."

What has happened is that over time these stories have become foundations of our personalities. If they tell us that we can't depend on anyone, we become "take-charge" types who often experience difficulties with trust and intimacy. If they say we must have firm beliefs about right and wrong, we live judgmentally, constantly assessing whether or not our friends and coworkers know what they are doing. If they say there's something wrong with us, we grow into adults who create elaborate compensatory behaviors to hide who we think we are. Our personalities come straight out of our stories whose themes become our "to-do" or our "not-to-do" lists.

Stories also remain invisible to us because we disguise them when we reaffirm them by constant repetition. A child whose parents were inattentive to her needs—for whatever reason—learned to suppress her needs and earn love and affection by never appearing to have any. Once that worked, she continues. She says to herself, "It must be okay because here I am today, doing what I did before, and tomorrow I will do it again." When we repeat our stories, they become familiar and feel right. It's a funny twist of the human psyche that we deal with our difficulties by repeating them.

Since we don't know that the stories direct our actions, we are powerless to find alternative solutions as we tell ourselves their themes over and over again in emotionally threatening situations. But given our tender ages and limited abilities when we created these solutions, these stories cannot possibly hold up in the long run. They are like ships we sail on that are off just a degree or two from where we want to go. At first, it's not noticeable and we still seem to be headed in the direction of love and attachment. But by the time years have gone by, that ship is nowhere near where we wanted it to be. A young child who learns not to get angry at her father grows into a woman who can only express hostility indirectly and self-destructively. As adults, we end up way off course, and the stories by which we navigated now stand in the way of our happiness and fulfillment and thus cause us pain. Once they explained reality, but now they keep us from being fully authentic and entire. The stories only become visible when our lives erupt in turmoil.

Ultimately, stories break down and stop working because they get in the way of the very things we want. It is impossible to be fully realized as an adult if we live by the conclusions of a child. It is impossible to experience real intimacy and connection if our actions are guided by fictions that instruct us to protect ourselves in the face of love and connection. When we live our lives according to humanity's greatest hits, we set off on a twisted path that ultimately can keep us from becoming truly authentic adults.

The challenge then becomes learning to know when a story is making the choices in our lives or when we are. We need to learn how to spot our fictions, picking them out and holding them up to the light of the present day and deciding whether or not their messages make sense for us anymore. To do that, it takes a lot of guts, frankly, because they are so interwoven with who we are and how we relate to the world.

Looking for Clues

Stories are great because finding them is like entering a wonderful detective novel. Each narrative has a clue in it about what the end of the book will be. But before we jump to the conclusion, we need to become adept at finding the clues themselves. Let's look at the most common stories I hear in my practice—humanity's greatest hits—and see if we can start to spot some clues about what is really going on. Since the first step on the path of becoming real involves knowing when a story is running the show and hiding the truth, we have to become adept at a new form of examination.

As you read through the following snapshots taken in the areas of love, money and work, and body image—the three main arenas of our lives—see if you can spot the needy child's story in each one. Once you start looking for stories in others' lives, it becomes much easier to find the ones dictating yours.

Stories of Love

If I were married (or married to the right person),
I'd be happy.

Angela gets very excited with each new date. Before dinner is over, she pictures herself in a wedding dress, looking lovingly into her date's eyes as they are about to pronounce their vows of love and devotion. The only problem is that by dessert, her date does something to prove he's not Mr. Right. The fantasy unravels, dashing her hopes and making her miserable. When she's not dating or when there's no new fantasy object on the horizon, she spends her time escaping into her imaginary wedding plans and the man who will complete her. Angela came to see me because she's in a downward spiral. She keeps dating married or unavailable men. She's terrified that life is going to pass her by—she'll never get married, never have kids, never belong anywhere. If she keeps this up, she might end up alone, but she just doesn't find available men interesting. Her story that she needs a man to be happy, along with her other story that only men who belong to other women are worth having, is leaving her feeling incomplete, lonely, and bad about who she is.

I'm just too needy.

Linda has been doing everything she can to find someone to spend her life with. She even tried a rapid dating service and spent six quality minutes with each prospective Mr. Right before she ran screaming into my office. She'd tried going to classes, frequenting bars, and even volunteering at a pet shelter, but in spite of her good looks and tremendous smarts, she can't meet anyone who wants to stick around. Each guy stays interested for a date or two but gets mysteriously busy pretty quickly—usually sometime after the first time they go to bed together. The most recent guy had stuck around longer than the rest—a month. But he broke up with her after she bought him a very expensive tie and then picked up the check at the romantic dinner she'd arranged. She sat in my office, stumped and miserable. "All I did was spoil him a bit," she sobbed. "I don't ask much for myself." Linda's story, her fear that she is so needy that she must do everything for herself and her partner (to fend off the giant pit of neediness that would overwhelm her partner and make him leave her) has made her totally controlling and unable to receive any giving—the kind of person who, frankly, no one wants to be with.

There's a right way and a wrong way to do everything,
and his way is wrong.

Laurie's husband drives her crazy. She says he's lousy in bed, he doesn't make enough money, and, on top of that, he's a slob. The other night when a few couples came to their house for dinner, he sat there with a big spot of salad dressing on his shirt and didn't lift a finger to help clean up. She felt beyond embarrassed—she had always been the envy of her friends for her dinner parties when she was single. Now, she can hardly bear to have them. She knows how to organize their home, their kids, and their money, but then he gets involved and it's all a big mess. This man is ruining her life. Laurie's story that she knows what is right and has to do it all her way is ruining both her own and undoubtedly her husband's enjoyment of and closeness in the marriage. If she maintains this story, she'll end up divorced.

I can't depend on anyone but myself.

Colleen announces that she's just not going to get married again—period. There is no one out there with a sense of duty and responsibility anymore. Her ex-husband had no sense of responsibility. He didn't pay the bills on time and had hurt their credit rating. He created chaos in the house, never knew where anything was and, no matter how much she bugged him, could not remember to do even the simplest things like sending a thank-you note to her mother for a birthday present. He couldn't even buy the right brand of fabric softener! It took so much out of her trying to get him to do the right thing that she'd finally given up. She just didn't want to have children with a man who was such a child himself. He'd seemed so carefree and spontaneous when she first met him. Little did she realize he was just a kid in a man's clothing. All she wanted was someone to take care of her once in a while. Was that so much to ask? Colleen's story that others are never dependable has left her unable to get the one thing she really wants, which is to be cared for in return. She could no longer enjoy her husband's spontaneity, and probably neither of them can remember why she fell in love with him in the first place.

All of these women may have legitimate complaints about the men— or lack thereof—in their lives. But look more deeply. They have all set up roadblocks to intimacy in their love lives even though each one is quite different. Ask them and they will quickly tell you that they aren't the problem, these guys are. But each of these women has handpicked these men, and they are acting out dramas that started early in childhood. By telling themselves these stories, though, they almost guarantee themselves that what they say they want, they will never get.

We will go deeply into the meaning of each of these stories in the next few chapters, but for now, just keep reading and see what strikes a chord with you.

Stories of Money and Work

If I'm not number one, then why bother?

Theresa's résumé is great, with one exception: She changes companies every few years. This time she's about to leave her job because she hasn't been made a vice president. "I'm not being given the credit I deserve. I was the one who spearheaded the big campaign that got the major client, but did I get credit? No." While I would be tempted to sympathize with her, her history of dissatisfaction tells me that she's not some hapless victim. She tells me that she's left each company because she felt underrated and underappreciated. Theresa's story, which is about her need to feel like number one because anything else feels like being nothing, prevents her from getting any satisfaction from her career. It's only about outside acknowledgment, never about inner pride and feelings of accomplishment. In addition, the acknowledgment can never be enough because her story will always remind her she should have done better.

If I were more successful, I'd be happy.

Amy never quite makes it to the level she thinks she should. In her fifteen years as a tax accountant in a big firm, she's never gotten beyond the associate level. She watched as others were promoted around her. Okay, there was the time when she took an extra month of leave after having her second child and she had written that letter no one was supposed to have seen protesting the firm's taking on a large tobacco company. But she'd shown up every day, hadn't she? Well, almost every day. Her new supervisor has just made it very clear to her that she's going nowhere unless she "gets on the bus" with the rest of the staff and performs beyond what's written in her job description. Amy thinks it's discrimination because she has kids and her boss doesn't. She knows her work is good. All she needs, she told her boss, is a little recognition as an incentive. Amy can't make peace with the compromises she has made between family and work because her story keeps telling her that getting the title at work is what makes her valuable. If she could feel valued from within and know that no one can really have it all, she might recognize that she has plenty to be happy about already.

People don't give me the credit I deserve.

Martha has always seen herself as the power behind the throne at her publishing company. She edits everything for her boss, the editor in chief. She does all his paperwork and deals with all his authors, but does she ever get any recognition? No! Her most recent performance review reflected "an attitude" issue. Her? Where would he be without her? After all, she had spent the last ten years making him look great, staying at the office most nights and many weekends. And now he's criticizing her because all she has done is make him look like a star. Martha's "attitude" is her story's conviction that she is never good enough and others exploit her. If she can stop seeing herself as a perpetual victim, then she can give herself the credit she deserves.

I can't do anything wrong or I'll pay.

Bridget is terrified of being in the office when her water breaks but is even more concerned about taking time off before giving birth to her first child. She's seen other women take advantage of maternity leave and feels that it was wrong of them. Worse than that, however, are her fears that she'll be made to pay if she takes the full six weeks allowable as stated in the company employee manual. Yet she also knows that time is critical for bonding with the baby. Two sets of rules, each set against the other. Bridget feels more than torn—she feels as if she's going to have a nervous breakdown trying to do the right thing in two places. In Bridget's world, right and wrong are black and white and she cannot see the grays. Her story doesn't work when there are two opposing rights—the right at work and the right of mothering. No matter what she does, she will be miserable unless she can see how her story is creating an artificial, one-dimensional view of right and then commanding that she do it.

My problems are my mother's fault.

Susan is furious. All her life her mother told her she could be anything she wanted. She could have a huge brain and still look like a million bucks. "Look at Ally McBeal," her mother had once said. But now, she feels betrayed. She has just been blind-copied on an E-mail that alleged she got her promotion because she looked like a hooker.

Well, who says she has to dress like a nun to be good in her job? The problem is that all the women in the office are pea green with envy because she is the one who always gets noticed. Her father—who was a huge business success—told her she had to dress with style. She doesn't hear any of her accounts complaining. Her sales were over her targets when everyone else was barely making theirs. So why is everyone accusing her of getting by on her looks? Isn't she allowed to have a brain and be feminine, too? Why hadn't her mother warned her? Had she secretly wanted to sabotage her? After all, she'd paid for most of Susan's clothes . . .

In Susan's story, her mother has set her up to be the target of all women's wrath, as well as a phony. Therefore, she can't believe in herself or have any true friends.

If I let them win, they'll like me.

Cathy came to see me on her Internist's recommendation. She had developed enormous and debilitating headaches that kept her from functioning. She missed so much work that her job was now in jeopardy. When I asked her what was going on, she told me she had a new boss at her online magazine. This man may have had an MBA, but he'd never made a creative decision in his life. Now, he was editing her copy and making assignments that made no sense to her. But she desperately wanted his approval and was terrified of losing her job in this uncertain economy. So she began doing everything he said. The magazine was losing so much money now that she feared they'd all lose their jobs, but she wouldn't say a word. Cathy believes that to be liked or loved she has to give in, particularly to authority. It costs her self-respect and it will cost her the job.

———————

Left unconscious, these are powerful scenarios that too often end in our self-destruction. We get so much of our identities from our work and measure ourselves by our jobs and our paychecks. It is so simple to blame the boss, blame the job, the profession, the economy. But each one of these examples shows how stories show up in our lives, whispering songs of entitlement, injustice, or lack of recognition. The tricky thing about work is that many companies and bosses do act in ways that might be considered unfair or even discriminatory, but that doesn't stop these setups from tapping into our deepest fears.

Stories of Body Images

If I were thinner, I'd be happy.

Beth recently got a promotion at work. Her oldest child was accepted to her first choice of colleges. On paper, everything in Beth's life looks great. But none of that is lifting Beth's mood. Instead, she is trapped in a loop of self-criticism. She can't stay away from the cookie jar. She had strategies: Just don't buy them (but what would the kids eat?). Or buy them and pour water over the ones she is tempted to eat. Or dump them under the coffee grinds in the trash. Or throw them up if she's had too many. Her little tricks aren't working anymore, and as a consequence, Beth has been gaining ten pounds a year for the past three years. Beth spends hours fantasizing about how she would look in the clothes she sees in store windows and catalogs. In her mind, she always looks amazing. But then she catches her reflection in a window or mirror. Looking back at her are saddlebags and a belly. She hates herself for the hours spent in some other imaginary body. Her sex life with her husband is almost nonexistent. She's too ashamed to get naked in front of him. But to be honest, he's not so hot to trot either these days. She's on her fifth diet in as many months, and it's all she can think about anymore. She knows that if she can just lose thirty pounds, all her problems will be solved—her husband would fall back in love with her and she'd take joy again from everything. Beth's story that her appearance is the key to happiness and being loved is likely what makes her eat in the first place. She will have to love herself before she can stop using food to comfort and yet destroy herself.

If I make a mistake, I'll be punished.

Melissa goes to the gym every day no matter what. She lives in fear of gaining back the weight she recently lost after her father told her she'd gotten too fat to find a husband. And it wasn't even that much— only twenty pounds. But now, if she doesn't get on the treadmill, she says she feels bad and can't eat. If she burns up 300 calories, she can have a bagel; 400 for a bagel and cream cheese. Melissa can tell the calorie count and fat content of every food known to humankind. Nothing goes in her mouth that she knows she can't work off the next day. Melissa feels like a bad person when she eats more calories than she's burned. Wracked with guilt, she starves herself or runs anxiously to the newest exercise class.

If I were thinner, younger, prettier, in better shape . . . if I had blond hair, blue eyes . . . if I were taller, shorter, less wrinkled—then I'd be happy, loved, complete. These statements pain me every time I hear them. The first thing we know is our bodies. As children we love them—they are the vehicles through which we see, touch, smell, taste, and hear the world and experience the ones we love so much. Our brains live in our bodies; our bodies express our love to others. Thus, it is the ultimate tragedy when we turn on the very thing that gives us life.

One of the saddest things about these stories is that, when we believe in them, they make our whole lives conditional. We live in a weird kind of "if/then" universe in which we will only be okay in certain situations. That means we spend massive amounts of time and energy creating those conditions that will make us feel comfortable, familiar, and safe—and massive amounts of energy denying that we actually created the situations that are making us so tired. If I were to tell any of these women above that they were not innocent victims of circumstance but instead agents of their own destinies, they would hand me my hat and show me the door. The unconscious protects our stories by making them invisible to us or making them appear to be "the truth."

It's very hard to look at our stories because we risk seeing things we don't want to see and feel things we don't want to feel. Stories work a bit like Pandora's box—when we open them, out come all the original and painful emotions that caused the stories' creation in the first place. That's why we go for so long with our lives out of whack before we are willing to look at our underlying fictions. I cannot tell you how many people I see in my practice who don't want to examine their marriages, because they risk realizing how ambivalently they feel about their spouses. Ambivalence creates too much anxiety for them, which is a problem because everyone has some mixed feelings about those they love. There is no intimacy without that. The story's goal is to squash this anxiety. Instead, people choose to live with a blind eye because the alternative means reexperiencing pains that come directly out of the frustrated primary needs.

But until we learn to spot our stories and then become willing to let them go, we will be locked into a cycle that will rob us of our dreams and drain us of our energies. If these women could understand that their stories are calling the shots in their lives, they would be free to chart a different path to what they want—one that doesn't take all the effort that went into creating the self-defeating situation in the first place. Imagine what they could do with all the energy that would be unleashed.

It's hard to believe that we put up with the chaos that outdated stories create. But there is comfort in them. Each time we find ourselves in the accustomed roles with rules we understand, we reaffirm an orderly universe in which we know how to operate. These are problems we understand how to solve—after all, we figured out how to get through these conflicts as young children. So what if our solutions aren't always the healthiest or don't bring us closer to discovering new strengths? They work for us. Even when we know that eating the cookie doesn't really make us feel better or pushing away help or snapping at our mothers before they can criticize us doesn't solve anything in the long run, we do these things because they have become second nature. Before we can get to that first nature, that real nature, though, we must first dismantle the structures our stories have built—our personalities.

Chapter Four

EVERY STORY CREATES A PERSONALITY TYPE: FIND YOURS

Andrea and her elder brother, Robert, are arguing bitterly about how to care for their ailing mother. Andrea, who was quite young when their father died, feels they owe it to their mother to have her live with one of them. Robert wants nothing to do with any of it and is all for putting their mother in a nursing home after her last stroke. "We came from the same parents, grew up in the same house, we were taught the same values," she says to me, shaking her head. "I just look at this guy and wonder how on earth we came from the same family."

Many of us marvel at how different our personalities can be from those of our siblings. Even though we grow up under the same roof with the same parents, we can end up radically different from each other. When we have kids of our own, we see that each child comes into the world with a distinct temperament. But personality differs from temperament. Who we become depends not only on that basic wiring but also largely on the stories that dominate us. Since, as we saw earlier, we use different stories to explain why we haven't had our primary emotional needs met, it stands to reason that we develop different ways of being in the world based on what felt absent in our lives.

Andrea has a caretaker-type personality, while her brother is more self-centered. The formative event in both their lives was their father's death. He died suddenly of a heart attack, leaving their mother with very little. The combination of a lack of money and two small children (Andrea was three and Robert was ten) stressed out their mother to the point of exhaustion. Her focus quickly shifted from raising her kids to keeping a roof over their heads. In each sibling's case, different emotional needs went unmet. Robert got the message from his mother that his interests had to be focused on being "the man of the house," and Andrea quickly learned that any need she expressed was a burden to her already overtaxed mother. Ultimately, Andrea's story created a caretaker, and Robert's created a rather self-centered man. I'm being somewhat simplistic here, but it's important to explain the connection between unmet or frustrated primary emotional needs and a person's ultimate personality. Depending on the story that comes out of those needs, a distinct personality evolves. The important thing to know is this: *Our stories largely determine our personalities.*

Why does this matter? For all the reasons in the world. As long as we react to the world through the prism of our stories, we will continue to follow the marching orders of a powerful unconscious that reacts to the world like the child who created the story in the first place. Stories don't update. They stay frozen in time. If your story tells you it isn't safe to get angry when you're five, you'll be telling yourself the same story at fifty unless you recognize it and rewrite it. These dictates may have given us a safe harbor because we used them to resolve the conflict between our primary needs and their lack of fulfillment. But as mature and independent grown-ups, these same stories limit our choices, our actions, and our lives. We have become who we are based on long-ago tales created for long-ago realities.

As we mature, our stories don't automatically correct themselves. Whatever we were compensating for as children remains with us as adults unless we intervene. I like to think of it like this: If, when we were young, we learned we couldn't use our right hands because every time we did it caused us pain, we would learn to use our left hands for everything. Slowly, this way of existing becomes natural to us and we build tremendous strength in our left arm muscles. One day, life hands us something that requires both hands. We face a decision: Drop the opportunity or learn to draw on greater strengths. Using our right hand is going to be awkward at first, maybe even painful. And we aren't going to have the faith that it can function. But if we want to grab life with all we've got, or get out of a rut we are in, or break a self-destructive way of living, we are going to have to become willing to examine our one-handed ways.

Our personalities function just like this. Take Andrea. She felt that there was no room for her needs during her father's illness and death and her mother's subsequent depression. So she learned two things: that her needs were too great to ask anyone to fulfill them and that she could still have love and connection but only if she took care of people whose love she desired. She anchored her story by integrating it into her identity. Originally constructed to avoid pain, over time, our subsequent personalities become limited—they have to be since they are built on our stories' mission of avoiding pain.

Because our stories and our personalities are so enmeshed, we are going to resist deep inspection. That's only natural. If someone walks up to you after a lifetime of living one-handed and says, "You can use both hands," the only sane thing to do is dismiss that person as nuts. It's just too threatening to have to contradict or abandon something that has worked well enough for you all these years and is the only way you know how to cope. But if someone tells you that your personality limits your ability to grow and change and solve current problems in your life, you might consider giving that person a hearing.

The path to real change lies through understanding our personalities. They are the expressions of our stories. If our stories tell us it's not safe to depend on anyone for support, our personalities are going to reflect a very independent person who asks no one for help and who can't even receive a gift from someone without feeling indebted. If our stories tell us there is a right or wrong way to do everything, we are going to be highly critical, judgmental, and exacting people.

As individual as we all are, our stories fall into certain patterns and types that come directly out of our primary emotional needs. While the variety is almost infinite, most people fall into one of five personality types determined by which need or needs went unmet. These types are:

- The Dependent
- The Superachiever
- The Self-defeater
- The Competitor
- The Perfectionist

Finding Your Personality Type

Personalities are like fingerprints—swirls and whirls and each one unique. I want to be very clear about something: I have never seen one person who was all one personality type or all another. This makes us rich and textured as people. That said, we all have a particular set of stories that dominates the rest and thus creates a dominant personality type. Below I'm going to give you a personality-type questionnaire. Answer "yes" or "no" in response to each question. You will probably recognize yourself in several situations, but do your best.

It's very difficult to know when our stories are determining our actions, so I've divided the questions into the three main areas in life where our personalities (and our collections of stories, the most common of which I call humanity's greatest hits) come out: love, work, and body image. Remember that we're dealing with stories that are invisible to us because they are creations of our unconscious minds. Our personalities grow right out of these stories and surface in our actions. The unconscious wants our personalities to be second nature. That unconscious mind works under our radars, which means that we can look right at a list of the five personality types and think, "No way, that's not me." Or "Well, I have some of this and some of that, so none of it applies." I have news for you: It *all* applies.

These questions are not to find out if you have a serious mental disturbance, but they are designed to help you discover your character style or personality type. You will likely find yourself in one or more of these five types. Once you determine which dominant personality you are (but read them all because I promise you, you have bits of each in you), you can start on the road that leads to separating your myth from reality. Think of the following personalities as building blocks that we all assemble in different and unique ways. None of us is built the same. You may identify with one story more than another. But *all* of us are built of the same material.

As you answer this questionnaire, here are a few things to keep in mind:

1. If your answer is "sometimes" or "maybe," count it as a "yes." We often hide our real feeling even from ourselves.

2. If you answer "yes" to two or more questions in a series, the personality type those questions correspond to applies to you. (Remember, we're often more than one type although one type is usually dominant.)

3. You may find that you aren't the same type in each category. If you are one type in love and another type at work, it simply means that you've got a few different stories going on. This is often the case. But pay attention to each category. Your story—whichever one it is—is dominating your behavior there.

Personality-Type Questionnaire

For each of the following questions, please answer "yes" or "no."

In your love relationships:

1. Do men always hurt you in the end?
2. Will you do anything to keep your partner from getting angry at you?
3. Does your partner often mistreat you?
4. Do you always submit to what your partner wants?

5. Does it seem your partner doesn't understand the rules of life?

6. Do you feel overwhelmed when your partner wants to do things differently from the way you do them?

7. Does your partner always seem to do things the wrong way?

8. Do all men seem really irresponsible?

9. Do you find yourself attracted only to married or otherwise un-available men?

10. Do you often date men who are much older than you?

11. Do you think that if you had the "right" man, you would then feel good about yourself and be happy?

12. Do you often feel attracted to your girlfriends' men?

13. Do you feel crushed if you are not the focus of your partner's at-tention, his number-one interest?

14. Is it hard to maintain interest in a man for any length of time?

15. Do you fantasize constantly about being romantically involved with larger-than-life people?

16. Once you are in a relationship, are you quickly disappointed with who your partner really is?

17. If you showed your partner what you really want and need from him, do you think that you would lose his love?

18. Do you feel compelled to do everything for your partner, but re-sent it deep down?

19. Do you end up working so hard in your relationship that you ul-timately collapse?

20. Do you feel you can never really depend on your partner?

Key: Yes to questions 1–4 is the Self-defeater, 5–8 is the Perfectionist, 9–12 is the Competitor, 13–16 is the Superachiever, and 17–20 is the Dependent.

At your job:

1. Do you feel no one gives you the credit you deserve?

2. Do you believe you could be a happy person only if you were the absolute star of the office?

3. Is being average devastating to you?

4. Is it torture doing the behind-the-scenes legwork, and do you only enjoy the front-and-center tasks that get a lot of recognition?

5. Are you always the scapegoat whenever there is trouble at work?

6. Do you do all the grunt work but get no appreciation for it?

7. Although it makes you miserable, do you always stay late and take on too much?

8. Do you worry a lot that a coworker is angry with you?

9. Do you feel there is only one right way to do the job?

10. Are you often frustrated with coworkers who keep making mistakes you have to correct?

11. Do you often feel anxious about making mistakes at work?

12. Do you spend a lot of time checking over your work?

13. Is it difficult for you to collaborate with others on a project?

14. If you work in a group, do you tend to do the lion's share of the work?

15. Does it make you nervous if you have to rely on a coworker for some of your work?

16. Do you wish that someone would take care of you so you would never have to work again?

17. Do you feel like no one thinks you're smart?

18. Do you feel you have to use your looks to get anywhere at work?

19. Do you flirt a lot with your superiors?

20. Does work get boring quickly if there is no physical attraction going on in the office?

Key: Yes to questions 1–4 is the Superachiever, 5–8 is the Self-defeater, 9–12 is the Perfectionist, 13–16 is the Dependent, and 17–20 is the Competitor.

About your body:

1. Do you feel you are so fat that no man will ever want you?
2. Do you often blame others for your struggles with your weight, hair, or state of health?
3. Do you tend to go on extreme diets (like starvation) and do extreme exercises that leave you in pain?
4. Do you have a lot of rules about what and how much you can eat or have to exercise?
5. Do you feel very nervous if you eat more than you "should" or if the scale goes up a pound?
6. Do you never think your body looks good enough?
7. Do you always work hard to look sexy but really don't enjoy sex much?
8. Do you think if you were thinner or prettier you would be able to hold on to your man or more men and that life would be much happier for you?
9. Are you terrified at the prospect of no longer being able to catch or keep a man with your looks?
10. Do you feel like nothing if you are not noticed by others when you enter a room?
11. Do you spend a lot of time thinking about or doing things to look

thinner, younger, more beautiful—such as plastic surgery or buying the many products that promise these things?

12. Do any "flaws" in your appearance devastate and preoccupy you?

13. Do you think a lot about getting sick?

14. Do you often get strange aches and pains that don't seem to be
due to a known illness?

15. If you get sick, do you find that you feel kind of relieved?

Key: Yes to questions 1–3 is the Self-defeater, 4–6 is the Perfectionist,
7–9 is the Competitor, 10–12 is the Superachiever, and 13–15 is the
Dependent.

You probably have a mix of types, but take a look at your answers
and see which type dominates. (And while you're at it, think about the
loved ones in your life—what type are they? Knowing the answer will
probably help you understand why they act and react in the sometimes
unfathomable and frustrating ways they do!) You will find that you're
probably (but not necessarily) going to be the same type for each area.
Even if you answered "yes" to only two of the four questions for that
personality type, it probably still applies to you. Don't worry about
the labels (remember these come out of hurts, and it's important to
have real compassion for yourself). They are being used only for the
purpose of understanding yourself. Remind yourself that you are on
the first step of the path that leads to the uncovering of your real,
authentic, mature self. Since each personality type comes from your
collection of stories and each of those comes from a perceived unmet
need, understanding the story's evolution allows you to go back and
update, rewrite, and break free of the invisible bonds that chain you to
your past.

The Five Personality Types

The Dependent

Alison is a beautiful redhead in her mid-forties with two kids and a marriage that's on the rocks. Her doctor referred her to me because she's begun to experience fainting spells and he can't find any physical reasons for them. "I've always been the strong one," she says to me. "I've been the chief wage earner. I take care of the kids. But I can't keep passing out like this. It's wreaking havoc on my life."

Rick, Alison's husband, has just told her he wants a separation. "I can't believe that now that I need him, he's leaving," she says. "I can't help these spells—how come when I need help, no one is ever there for *me*?"

There it is—one of the hallmarks of the Dependent personality—the feeling that it's not safe or even possible to ask for or depend on another person. Indeed, as I learn more about her, Alison's personality is a pretty classic example of the Dependent. On the surface, she's extremely independent (I'll explain the paradox here in a minute), she's strong, and she focuses on others' needs often at the expense of her own. While these are marvelous, generous attributes, they aren't so selfless. Dependents care for others because they fear no one will care for them. They feel like bottomless pits of neediness inside but fear that, if someone finds that out, they will be abandoned. So they develop almost impenetrable independent shells.

This personality type comes out of the first primary emotional need—to attach and bond. When something happens to frustrate that bonding, it sets the stage for a person, like Alison, who is too afraid to let herself depend on or look to another person for love and attachment. Because this need happens so early in life, when it's frustrated, we experience intense and preverbal fears of being abandoned or unloved. So Dependents compensate unconsciously for their fears and hurts by telling themselves these stories:

- I can do it alone.
- I can't depend on anyone else.
- No one ever takes care of me.
- My needs are so great, they will overwhelm anyone who sees them.
- My needs are unrealistic.
- If I express my needs, I will be abandoned and rejected.
- I'm selfish and I want too much.

In the most common stories, Dependents have trouble with relationships because they aren't capable of asking for help. While Dependents excel at giving, they can't let others give to them. Real intimacy demands give-and-take. This personality is an outwardly "take charge" one. They usually become caretakers because their own bonding was frustrated. In Alison's case, her mother was diagnosed with breast cancer shortly before she was born. Immediately after Alison's birth, her mother underwent surgery and chemotherapy. Alison experienced this abandonment by equating her needs with someone else's pain. As time went on, this association didn't change—only the cast of characters did. She never felt comfortable showing anyone how much she needed love because her story told her that her love would cause others pain and result in her own rejection. Not surprisingly, in spite of her friendliness, warmth, and charm, Alison was never able to ask for what she most wanted—to be taken care of.

Instead, Dependents like Alison develop an ability to get their needs met indirectly by vicariously enjoying the fulfillment of other people's needs. Their sense of well-being depends on the well-being of others.

The only way Dependents ever feel free to let others take care of them is when they are very sick or incapacitated. This explained Alison's fainting spells to me. Because they feel they can't ask for anything, Dependents often end up with chronic physical problems—they get ulcers or back pain, mind-numbing headaches, or overwhelming physical exhaustion so severe that they finally allow themselves the care they so desperately crave.

In a sad twist, whoever does try to take care of a Dependent in a period like this usually comes out of the experience feeling they just couldn't do enough to help. Feeling dependent is so emotionally charged for this personality type that the actual experience of relying on someone creates profound anxiety and discomfort. As a consequence, they can't acknowledge how great it is to be taken care of at last. Instead, they respond ungraciously because they feel their endless neediness will drive away the person caring for them and because it makes them feel like "bad" people for wanting the care in the first place.

The relationship between caretaking and attachment goes beyond any kind of ego gratification in the Dependents' world. There's an urgency to their actions because they feel that if they don't care for others, they will be abandoned. They want love and affection so much, but in their minds, love equals loss. Attachment becomes so painful to them, so horrible, that they depend only on themselves. Deep inside, they feel there must be something wrong with them. Their stories tell them that it must have been their overwhelming needs that caused the abandonment and rejection, so they become people who live by the motto: "I don't need anyone. I will do it all myself."

Ultimately, Dependents tend to be loners. On the surface, they may be very outgoing types with many acquaintances, but they allow few if any close friends. Or they get involved with people they can't ultimately spend their lives with—like married men or men in different time zones. They stay away from relationships because they can't tolerate the differences that rise up between people because they feel too much like abandonments. While others can say, "You're separate and that's okay, you still love me and I still love you," such a sentence does not fall from the mouths of Dependents. Any disagreement feels like an abandonment for this personality type, so if you're looking for a good knockdown-dragout fight, turn elsewhere. Most of the time, Dependents will avoid conflict and won't engage in arguments. They will simply withdraw.

Dependents also feel tremendously conflicted about being close to people because their extreme neediness leaves them without the ability to create healthy boundaries. When they connect to someone, they often feel like they are being taken over and eaten alive. This makes perfect sense since connection is synonymous with caretaking. This creates a double jeopardy situation where the Dependents' happiness depends on people pleasing, which in turn drains them emotionally and physically and also makes them question whether or not the objects of their affection would love them if they weren't so well taken care of. It's a heartbreaking dilemma, and it's most often solved by avoiding any situation that even whispers the possibility of creating it.

Being around Dependents isn't always easy. They buzz around you, finish your sentences, repeatedly ask you if you need something or want something. Their needs have become focused completely on fulfilling yours. Like Alison's marriage, things stop being a two-way street. Her husband, Rick, felt he had no place in the relationship because part of the joy of marriage is giving to your partner and fulfilling her needs. Because he was denied this role, Rick never felt that Alison needed him, and on the rare occasions when she did, he never felt that what he did was done correctly or adequately. This followed them into the bedroom where he never got the ecstasy of giving her pleasure or an orgasm. She withheld that from both of them.

Alison didn't have a "real" relationship with Rick because she managed everything by holding back so she wouldn't experience—and Rick wouldn't see—her extreme neediness. She cut herself off from the joy that comes from having someone else fill you up. If she could see her story, then she might be able to ask Rick for help. She would not live with the constant fear that she would overwhelm him and he would abandon her, leaving her alone for good. Sad to say, her own attempts at managing the relationship created exactly the result she most feared.

The Superachiever

Andrew's eight-year-old son, Adam, has developed a tic—he blinks repeatedly whenever he feels under any pressure. "He reminds me of the way I was as a kid," Andrew tells me. "I was just like him. I had to have my homework done perfectly and if I even got one answer wrong on a spelling test, I cried."

Andrew thinks his wife, Junie, blames him for Adam's temperament. He tells me that the other night she snapped, "What happened during your psych classes? Did you ever think Adam's problems might have something to do with your endless need to be number one? These things are only as hereditary as your actions."

To tell the truth, Andrew does fear he's looking at a case of "like father, like son." He looks at me, hoping I'll contradict him, but I don't say anything immediately because he's not wrong.

Junie has had it with her husband, especially now that his behavior seems to be hurting Adam. Their marriage has been on the rocks for the past six months, and she's asked Andrew to start seeing me in the hope that I will be able to help him move beyond his constant feelings of being criticized. She tells him that it's not just his inability to listen to any criticism that's pushed her to her wit's end, but his superior, judgmental, and dismissive behavior toward her. She doesn't want any part of it anymore, and she really doesn't want her son growing up with this behavior as the model for a relationship. Andrew just doesn't see it, but, given what's at stake, he's become willing to look.

It hadn't always been that way between them; when Junie and Andrew met, she thrilled him. She was an artist, and her nonconformity gave Andrew the perfect outlet for his rebellion against his mother. This was not the country-club girl from a "good" family Andrew's mother had hoped for her track-star, Ivy-League, top-of-his-class surgeon of a son. No, half African-American and half Filipino, Junie was about as far from his mother's ideal as possible.

Andrew had loved, too, Junie's lack of orthodoxy, her impetuousness, her very differentness. While he ground away at college, medical school, and surgical residencies, she was a free spirit who had dropped out of college to travel the world. Early on in their relationship, she was seen as one of the up-and-coming young artists. But slowly over their married years, he's seen her drift toward convention—now channeling her creativity into children's projects and home décor. She no longer entrances him, and indeed she does seem as uninformed and irrelevant in her opinions as his mother did.

Now, Andrew feels judged by his wife, this wife who hasn't even worked a day in her life. This woman who hasn't finished college. This woman who once seemed to accept him without question. She blames Adam's need to be perfect on him. Who is she to say such a thing? If there was any mental instability, it certainly wasn't from his side of the family. Added to this is the fact that Andrew is pretty sure that his son is as brilliant as he is—he could also become an accomplished surgeon. Junie doesn't seem to understand that Adam needs to have straight As—how could she from *her* background? He has to be the best; he must excel to achieve his potential and be happy. Andrew praises Adam every time he does well—either in class or in sports—but he overrides Junie's objections and comes down on Adam when he falls short of the mark. Andrew tells Junie that this kind of guidance is for Adam's own good: "It's what made me my best, and my son can also be the best. My father may have had many faults, but he was a huge success and he knew something about raising one. I'm just passing it along."

Andrew has retreated into recrimination. He is enraged with Junie for pointing a finger at him, and I caution him that an unwillingness to look at the situation will not only hurt their marriage but will also hurt their son. All Andrew can see is how hard he has worked and how much he has provided for his family. His sense of injustice overwhelms him.

Andrew is a classic Superachiever. He can't handle any criticism; he can't have any weaknesses or failings. The moment he feels he isn't at the top of the heap, he immediately deflates to nothing. The Superachiever's story begins when the need to become a separate individual becomes frustrated. When a child goes off to explore and become a separate self, what happens? In some cases, the parent feels comfortable enough with who they are and who their child is to support the enterprise. The Superachiever is created, however, when a child has a parent who either has such a high estimation of her that she feels she can't possibly live up to it or the parent wants or expects something different from what that child's real self is.

When this happens, the message the child gets is that who she is isn't "right." As a result, she tries to become the person her parent esteems. In doing so, she stops valuing the person she really is, and a gulf opens between that authentic personality and the one that she thinks will get her love and approval. The child will need to maintain this new personality for years in order not to disappoint her parent and, later, herself.

Superachievers exist even in families where there is tremendous love. Jenna's mom praised her repeatedly for being a tremendous brain who was clearly going to be doctor or lawyer. But Jenna was actually a very quiet and placid kid who was smart enough, but was more interested in drawing and painting than spelling-bee competitions. Jenna saw that her mother expected her to compete and excel. In order to make her proud and ensure her continued love, this naturally contemplative and somewhat introverted kid not only tried to be what she imagined her mother wanted but also learned to value that person more than her real self. As a little kid, Jenna couldn't say, "Mom, this is the way I am, like it or lump it," so understandably she began to bury who she was and become what Mom thought she was.

Unfortunately, there is a built-in feedback loop here, because as long as Jenna did all those things her mother loved, she was going to keep praising her. She learned to seek that reinforcement, which began a vicious cycle that would last her a lifetime. Both Jenna's and Andrew's stories are unforgiving and exacting.

Superachievers grow up saying to themselves:

- I must be perfect, special, omnipotent.
- I have to be able to know things without learning them.
- I must achieve things without working at them.
- I have a magical specialness.
- If I'm not number one, then I'm nothing at all.

This magical thinking is infused with an urgent immediacy—a need to be powerful and universally admired. The Superachiever survives on admiration because it confirms that she's lovable. If she makes a mistake, she plunges headlong into feelings of worthlessness, nothingness, and self-loathing. This personality type exists in a most polarized world, careening back and forth between feeling superspecial and worthless.

Because the Superachiever needs so much external reinforcement, we often look at them and think of them as selfish narcissists who suck up all the air in a room, squash any debate or challenge, and act superior. But if we could crawl inside their heads, we would hear the theme from their stories intoning, "The world is only safe if I'm a good person. I'm fundamentally broken. If I'm not perfect, I'm worthless." In reaction to that internal message, these people tend to dominate those around them.

Our society is more accepting of men like this than of women. The puffed-up "I am perfect" stuff can be viewed as highly successful and macho for men on the way up the ladder of success, while in women it is often viewed as bitchy and self-centered.

Not surprisingly, there are a lot of dictators among Superachievers. They tend to be very superior and very rigid, and they need to have things a certain way. They walk around with the fantasy of "I can do anything. I am the greatest." They may not even realize that this myth is a desperate run from "I am nothing. I am a little girl who not even my mommy could love."

Superachievers are heartbreaking because their stories create personalities that are often hard to like. No one enjoys being put down, and, unfortunately, Superachievers often criticize those around them to feel merely adequate themselves. The Superachiever story makes someone in so much need often deeply unappealing. Sadder still is the fact that Superachievers often hand down their stories to the next generation. If I were to bet on Adam's future personality, I would guess he will have a personality very much like his father's.

The Self-defeater

Lisa's father is driving her up the wall. She's fed up with his overbearing and controlling manner, and as far as she's concerned, he's just made the last crack she's ever going to listen to about her inadequate life. He seems to work on three speeds—her weight, her career, and her lack of a husband. One's too much, one's too little, and the last is nonexistent. She's dying to tell him where he can go and, when he gets there, what he can do with his obsessive need to point out her shortcomings. He's just pointed out that she's about to turn forty-one, and his birthday wish for her is that next year her hypothetical boyfriend be the one to take her out to dinner, not her father.

Lisa feels the anger rising inside her, the heat in her cheeks, the pressure in her chest. Grimacing, she pushes away from the dinner table just a tiny bit too abruptly and stands to clear the dishes in order to go into the kitchen and breathe. Ever since her mother's recent death from lung cancer, the burden of taking care of her father has fallen completely on Lisa. Her older brother lives across the country and is too busy with his life to be of any use whatsoever. Still exhausted from the eighteen months of the nursing and radiation and therapy she went through with her mother, all Lisa wants from her father is an acknowledgment of her profound contributions to his life and her mother's care. On the one hand, she knows she isn't going to get it, but, on the other hand, she still keeps looking for that moment when she will get the recognition she craves.

When her mother was alive, everything was better, she thought, draining her wineglass at the kitchen counter. Her mom contained her father and minimized his expression of constant disappointment. But now, it was just the two of them face-to-face across the dinner table. In the three months since her mother had died, Lisa had gained ten pounds on top of the fifteen she already had to lose—something she knew galled her father. He seemed to be obsessed with her weight, but a nice dinner and a glass of wine felt like her only refuge. The more she ate, the more he nagged. But Lisa was just too tired to take her father on directly, and besides, every time she did, he managed to turn everything back on her anyway and make it her fault. Or she'd feel so badly about blowing up at him, so what was the point of getting angry? It was so much easier to just go along to get along.

Lisa was beginning to wonder what it was about her that made people take advantage of her. Just last week at work after months of working on the background and research work of a huge presentation, she wasn't even invited to the meeting with the client. She was angry with herself for not speaking up at the time, but she knew that it wouldn't have made any difference, so why rock the boat?

Lisa is a Self-defeater. Rather than stick up for herself with her father, she stuffs her anger at his disapproval through food and alcohol. Rather than asserting her right to be in on the presentation of her work, she just sits in self-pity. Self-defeaters may start with parents who don't give them the approval and support they need as they individuate, but as the years go on, they take on the task of being critical and self-sabotaging.

We all know Self-defeaters—they snatch defeat out of the jaws of victory. They suffer silently. They self-destruct. Their behavior makes us want to slap them sometimes, because there's nothing more infuriating than being around people who always need us to act badly so they can star as the victims in the disappointing stories of their lives. This behavior often applies to all the areas of a Self-defeater's life. Work, love, friendships—once someone's story directs them to punish themselves (and indirectly others) with self-abuse, love opportunities are lost, promotions vanish, and all sorts of health problems appear.

This personality begins when a child needs to express herself and meets with the message, "What you are feeling, thinking, saying, and doing is wrong." This differs from the Superachiever in an important way: Even though their stories both come out of feeling a lack of recognition and approval, the Self-defeater hears that her very essence is intolerable and incorrect.

There are parents who—because of their own stories—cannot tolerate difference or anger, and when they meet up with an individualistic child or an angry and defiant kid, it threatens them so much they feel compelled to squash any opposition from that child in words or deeds.

When Lisa was small, her father could not handle any conflict. The message given to her when she'd get angry was "I will not tolerate any dissension from you." Terrified of losing her father's love, Lisa quickly equated her outbursts with self-hatred. Over time, she became much too afraid of being abandoned by her father to risk even the slightest noncompliance.

A Self-defeater's story has the following messages:

- Who I am and what I feel are wrong.
- Anger is unsafe.
- If I'm a doormat, everything will be okay.
- I need to be "good" so everyone will like me.
- I can't take it when someone's mad at me.
- If I let them win, they'll like me.

It takes a lot of internal strength and self-possession for a grown-up to be able to convey the balanced message that while a child's behavior may not be okay—everything from disrespect to biting, kicking, etc.—her anger is okay and natural. Lisa's father was far too stressed out to accommodate any defiance. But the parent who in signal and in voice conveys the message "How dare you even feel angry at me? I will not tolerate any sort of breaking ranks!" inadvertently creates a rough choice for that child: Either they continue to resist and risk losing the source of love and care or they become extremely passive, taking the implied criticism deeply to heart.

So, what do these Self-defeater types say to themselves? "Okay, I give up. I will be good." Their very natural anger never goes away, however. It becomes subverted and sequestered somewhere within, and a smoldering story of passive resistance begins: "I will never give in," it whispers. "I'm going to show you. And the way I'm going to show you is by punishing you by withholding from both of us."

We all know people who find gratification in keeping their affections to themselves, realizing that this deprivation is going to hurt the other person more than it's going to hurt them. The Self-defeater actually finds some pleasure in this—this withholding gives them power and control. The dynamic creates the passive aggressive, the manipulator, the spiteful person. Outwardly, they may appear to be crying, "Woe is me, I'm always being controlled!" but they have ways of actually being very effective in this area. Self-defeaters can make you feel incredibly guilty when they resist in their indirect ways.

But this personality type appears much less harsh when we realize that the story comes from the Self-defeaters' desperate contract. They are willing to trade their own desires in exchange for connection. They say to themselves, "If I just do whatever anyone asks me to do, no one will leave me." This person's whole life is so tenuous. They feel that if they say the wrong thing or get angry, their lives will be unfixable and they will be abandoned and totally, utterly alone. Needless to say, this continual suppression of their natural wishes and needs creates a great deal of anger.

This smoldering rage leads to the Self-defeaters' other defining characteristic: chronic guilt about their hostile thoughts. Instead of letting themselves get angry, they passively encourage unkind or dismissive behavior toward themselves. They excuse this behavior, saying to themselves, "I deserve to be treated badly. After all, I have angry thoughts." Self-defeaters cannot express any hostility at all without blaming themselves for having brought on whatever made them angry in the first place. They are martyrs, sacrificing themselves so both they and those around them will suffer.

So, what happens? They implode with guilt. They take the struggle inside. They simultaneously feel anger and guilt. This dynamic sets up a horrible inner conflict that is most often resolved by a self-defeating act like compulsive eating, sex, or spending. They behave in self-sabotaging ways that invite others to criticize them, dismiss them, yell at them, or ignore them. That's their only emotional option. They are convinced that if they ever showed anyone the rage inside them, those people would run away for sure. Thus, they learn to react to others indirectly. Self-defeaters will turn around and act out the anger on themselves. They will cut off their own noses to spite *your* face.

The Competitor

"If I were only thinner, my life would be so much better," Ann says. At forty-one, she's a slightly brassy blonde with a pretty obvious nose job. Now she's thinking of getting her breasts reduced—a procedure she clearly does not need. Sadly, Ann has reduced her problems to her thighs and breasts. And then, there's the fact that she's a business success. "Guys just can't handle it if you're too smart or too successful," she says. If she were less intelligent, if her thighs were smaller, she wouldn't be single.

Her father has always been her biggest supporter and one-man fan club. She could count on him to stick up for her whenever her mother criticized her eating habits or suggested she really should cover her midrift at her age. "Nonsense," her father would respond. "Men like a girl with some meat on her—more to hold on to." He'd wink at Ann, and later she'd hear her parents arguing. In her family, Ann belonged to her father—a Daddy's girl—and her sister, Becky, belonged to her mother. As her father focused more on her, he became the one interested in her boyfriends, not her mother. He took her shopping for sexy clothes when she had a big date coming up. Her mother was less outgoing—more like Becky. When Ann would tell her father that she thought her mother didn't care as much about her as her sister, he would say, "Nonsense. She's just jealous of us. She doesn't understand you the way I do. She's not like us." Over the years, Ann watched her mother slowly become more distant and her father step in closer as her confidant and self-appointed soul mate.

But Ann can't think about that now—she's completely depressed because of what happened at her younger sister's wedding.

It's so shameful that she doesn't even want to think about it. Feeling sorry for herself, Ann had gotten drunk and danced until her heel broke and she fell on her ass in front of everyone. The next morning, she had woken up in bed with the best man, who, just by looking at her, made it immediately clear he didn't remember her name. But Ann did remember that he'd come to the wedding with someone else, and it took days to shake off her humiliation and guilt.

Ann has decided that this is the last wedding she'll ever go to that isn't hers. "All the good men are married," she states, "and at my age, the ones who aren't are such damaged goods. Or they can't handle my independence. If only I had a husband, my life would be complete."

In Ann's story, happiness is impossible—although she doesn't see that yet. With her, life's a competition with herself and with other women. Her entire self-worth is defined by male attention. She has to look great to get a guy. If she wins (slims down and succeeds), she still loses because she will always know that he's only interested in her for her body. If she doesn't, she loses because she's not sexy or enticing or pretty enough. But to feel good about herself, she needs the approval and reinforcement that only a man can provide. Everything is about getting the man. But she's beginning to see that she can't win either way.

Ann can't have an authentic relationship with her sister because it's all about winning and losing there, too. Anything her sister got was something Ann was denied. Anyone who likes her sister doesn't like Ann. It's all zero sum for her. She gets it all or she gets nothing. There is nothing in between.

This dynamic leaves her excruciatingly lonely. She feels no one knows her, and because everything hinges on her appearance, she can't let anyone know her insides. This leaves her feeling flimsy and inadequate because, according to this equation, her brain doesn't matter, only her body. She feels like a fairly despicable person because she really does understand the implications of her behavior—she really wants to win, and she knows that makes someone else lose. But win what? The love of someone who, in the end, makes her feel morally disgusting. Winning ensures she really cannot love herself.

Unlike the other personality types, the Competitor is usually a woman. The Competitor's story starts at the stage where a child needs an attuned relationship. She needs to be seen for who she is in her entirety and understood. She needs to feel accepted for who she is. But a Competitor personality starts when the relationship between a father and daughter is not attuned but is sexually inappropriate and the mother doesn't step in—for whatever reasons—to correct the situation. There's an enormous range of behavior here—from the inadvertent to the intentional. The father can be either outright seductive, overly suggestive in his behavior or his related exploits, or just plain boundary-less. This personality type gets its start much later than the previous three—right around the time when a girl starts budding as a young woman. Sexual abuse does not have to create it—although that is certainly a classic source. It can simply be that the father was overly interested in his daughter's development and very exhibiting of himself, talking explicitly about his sexual exploits or asking about hers. I've had patients whose fathers bought them sexy nighties or who were just extremely crass.

So how does this girl get her love? She has a very different problem from the other personality types because pleasing one parent in this situation usually means alienating the other. If her mother allows the dynamic to go on, she can get angrier and colder as the girl gravitates to the heat of the love of her father. And the girl can become enraged with the mother for not stepping in and helping her. Not surprisingly, the Competitor personality type is rife with problems involving sexuality, competition, and guilt. She has sexual problems because she believes deep inside that the man is only interested in her appearance and doesn't care who she is. She's competitive because she needs the love and attention of her father, but it comes at the cost of losing her mother. She feels guilty and sees herself as a horrible person. As with most Competitors, she blames herself for creating her situation.

Down the line, as they become sexual beings, Competitors feel sex is bad, dirty, even emotionally dangerous—although these feelings may be invisible to them. They are unable to be comfortable with their sexuality because it feels wrong. Because of the "me or her" choice they felt they had to make between their parents, any whiff of competition becomes intolerable. To win the affection of one parent meant the exclusion of the other. Thus the story evolves—Competitors feel they must either exaggerate or deny their sexual and competitive natures. That is the conflict that determines their lives.

With Competitors, you find the classic seductress—the woman who is flirty and sultry and very male focused. People look at her and think "Wow. Men must really go for her. She must be amazing in bed." A more likely scenario, however, is that once this woman's clothes are off, she is totally inhibited because (1) she feels sex is wrong or even incestuous, and (2) she feels profound guilt at having divided her parents.

As much as she hates it, a Competitor feels compelled to keep acting out her male magnet role because her story tells her that's what got her the acceptance and affirmation she needed. Sexuality may feel frightening to her because the emotional stakes are so high (because success carries losses), but her personality is based on using her looks to get the love and attention she needs. Not surprisingly, this woman's happiness depends disproportionately on having the "right guy," looking the right way, and having the right wedding dress.

The Competitor's story tells her these messages:

- I need a man to be happy.
- If only I were thinner/younger/prettier, my life would be better.
- Sex is damaging.
- Men are only interested in my body.
- There must be something wrong with me because no one stays around.

Later in life, the Competitor has tremendous problems with aging. Looking very young and very sexy is all that makes her feel okay. The first wrinkles and the arrival of cellulite make her feel there is nothing left for her. She fears growing older, knowing that each sign of advancing age renders her increasingly worthless.

It's understandable that Competitors pay a steep emotional price for any kind of emotional involvement. This is a deeply conflicted personality type. If someone finds them attractive by implication, someone else gets hurt. On the one hand, they feel compelled to compete for the love that the opposite sex gives; but, on the other hand, they feel like they can't really love or be sexual or be competitive, because what will happen? They get no mom. Competitors have a tremendous fear of being exploited and rejected for good reason—because they were as kids.

The Perfectionist

Emily stood in the middle of her daughter's room absolutely enraged. Julie had taped a poster of her favorite band to the wall in defiance of her mother's strict edict that nothing was to go on the wall. Period. Moving to the closet, Emily yanked open the door only to find dirty socks, underwear, a damp towel, and a pile of clean laundry all jumbled together on the floor. This girl was not getting with the program, Emily growled to herself. There would be consequences.

Emily had tried to drum into her daughter the importance of being responsible for her things. Learning the right way to do things had become much more important, too, as Emily suspected Julie's friends came from homes that were considerably more chaotic than hers. Recently, she'd dropped Julie off at her best friend's house only to hear music blaring from upstairs, while the girl's mother and brothers yelled at one another from floor to floor. Julie was spending a lot of time at her friend's house these days where sporting equipment and backpacks dotted the entryway floor like boulders.

No, this act of rebellion with the poster wouldn't do. Emily left a note for Julie that said that she'd better clean her room and do her homework ASAP or face some serious consequences.

Emily was exhausted from trying to counteract what she felt was going on in her preteen daughter's world. Life with her husband, Gary, was difficult enough—his half-hearted approach to making a living embarrassed Emily profoundly. All her friend's husbands had real drive and ambition and seemed so much more accomplished. But Gary had been so perfect when they were young—he'd grown up in the right church, gone to the same country club, and attended a superb college. He knew the little things that counted—like lining his silverware up on the plate to signal to a waiter at a restaurant that he'd finished eating. She marveled at how intimidated she'd been by his knowledge of opera and symphony. All that was fine, but he just hadn't taken his role as a husband and provider to heart, and she felt she'd never get over her resentment.

Now, she was at a loss. Emily felt she had to shoulder the burden of raising their daughter alone. She especially resented that she had to be the enforcer—showing Julie that there was a right way to do things and trying to tell her that people would appreciate and esteem her for it in the long run. Emily began to feel bitter and tired and all alone. But she shook off the feelings, knowing that she had to compensate for Gary if Julie was going to have a chance in this world.

The Perfectionists owe their personalities to growing up in a highly rigid or moralistic environment. A Perfectionist is born when a child looks to her family, friends, teachers, and loved ones for both guidance and acceptance but instead finds that both are highly conditional on correct behaviors. These children wish to understand and be understood, to appreciate and be appreciated, to tolerate and be tolerated.

But instead of finding a multi-textured world, they walk into systems where the world works in black-and-white terms—good and bad, right and wrong, moral and immoral.

The Perfectionist's conflict begins when she feels a myriad of emotions and wants to explore different ways of living but her surroundings will only tolerate one way of behaving. What does she do with her own varied sense of self? She feels, "I must have done something wrong. *I* must be wrong. I need to do the *right* thing to be loved."

Some kids are born naturally more sensitive than others, too, and are more vulnerable to the judgments their loved ones make about "right" or "wrong." These children are particularly susceptible to becoming Perfectionists—they hold themselves to very high standards. They don't accept anything less than top performance in themselves. They become workaholics. They have little compassion for those who don't work as hard as they have to excel. Somewhere, somehow, they got the message that life is very conditional—and to be okay and lovable, you better be right! Whenever a child grows up in a highly rigid moral environment, chances are, they will display Perfectionist qualities as an adult.

Since most Perfectionists grow up in highly controlled environments, it is not surprising that they learn to equate order with feeling safe and secure. They experience random events as chaos, and it unnerves them. Losing control truly terrifies Perfectionists because anything that teeters off the line will potentially catapult them into exile. To survive, they become extremely controlling of themselves and others.

The messages Perfectionists receive are:

- There's a right way and a wrong way to do everything.
- Rules are important and must be observed.

- I have to be perfect, or something bad will happen.
- I have to keep control of myself and others.

As little children, Perfectionists can be the bosses of the playground, but as adults, they become highly judgmental and critical. They react out of proportion to the slightest changes in schedules or routines. They become flooded with insecurity if their performance doesn't match up to their high standards. They also feel constricted—unable to be impulsive, joyous, or expressive. They suffer so much from their rulebound natures that are also highly, punitively self-critical. They are compelled to finish what they start and to make sure everything is in its right place. The sad thing about this personality type is that it often creates another Perfectionist because of the overwhelming needs for regimentation and exactitude.

Emily's rigidity can't be doing much to help her marriage—that's for sure. And it will certainly drive her teenage daughter away from her. Teenagers need to be separate and sometimes opposed to their parents if they are to find their individual selves. But Emily will interpret this as an intolerable breaking of the rules that means loss of respect and love. In her attempt to impose her internal dictates on her daughter, she will not only alienate her but possibly make relationships with "bad" people seem more appealing; there will be no open door for communication and nonjudgmental advice. Emily feels it's her "duty" to instruct Julie about the right and wrong of each situation, an approach that guarantees her daughter will either reject the relationship with her mother and not communicate at all or align herself with her mother, becoming the same suffering Perfectionist. Emily has already lost the openness of a real relationship with her husband, and her daughter is not far behind. Her story keeps her from experiencing any flexibility, joy, or pleasure in reaching high, reaching out, trying something new—even being a little "bad" once in a while and occasionally breaking some rules for fun.

Emily only feels safe in a world where things are good or bad. She is caught under the weight of these moral stones that also block any appreciation of how varied she could be. She lives as the harshest judge in her own court, and she must toe the line or receive her own sentence.

Emily never gets to experience the real exhilaration of trying something new or risky. No one can live up to her rules, so everyone and everything disappoints her. It's hard to love someone who's chronically disappointed in you, and if she keeps it up, she will eventually drive her husband and daughter away. Emily's story has created a personality that is stealing her chance at happiness.

Our Personalities Are Faulty Shields

This is tough stuff, looking at our personalities. That's why we don't do it unless we're in so much pain as a result of our behaviors that we have to change. But it gets a little easier when we realize that these personalities are nothing but faulty shields we used to fend off the disappointments, betrayals, and abandonments we felt when our primary emotional needs weren't recognized or met. When we stop and realize that all of it boils down to a spectacular effort on each of our parts to stay connected to love and security, it softens our own judgments about ourselves.

As hard as it is, however, one of the marvelous things about being an adult is that we can choose to unfold from the pretzel shape we bent into as children to ensure we received the care we needed to survive and connect directly and strongly to those we love in our lives. We are miles from where we were when our stories began. As adults, we have the ability to move out from under our false personalities and risk finding the real people we are underneath when we aren't protecting ourselves from old hurts.

I hope you can see something of yourself or someone you love in these personality types. If you can, you will be able to become conscious of when you are acting out old messages. No one comes out of childhood without inner conflicts. No one gets to adulthood without paying the consequences of the behaviors that come from personalities based on the unmet needs of long ago. When you see how your personality grew directly out of efforts to explain or resolve these painful conflicts, then you can begin the process of breaking free of their constraining hold on your life.

Chapter Five

WHEN YOUR STORY DEFEATS YOU

Martine came into my office utterly defeated. She had been so sure this time. Steve had seemed so different. He was the strong, silent type—artistic, independent, creative. He meditated. He washed the dishes. He was sensitive to her moods, and he taught her things about pleasure she'd never even thought possible. In short, he was nothing like any of the other men she'd ever dated, all of whom had one thing in common—at the end of the day, they had all treated her condescendingly and cruelly. Steve was different, or so it had seemed.

The first time Steve snapped at her, she was shocked. All she had done was suggest an alternative to the evening plans he'd proposed—she didn't want to go out; she wanted to stay home, order Chinese food, and watch a movie. "Christ Almighty," he said. "I have never met a woman with less imagination in my life." He'd hit Martine below the belt, right in the center of her insecurities—she secretly felt she *was* dull. She'd never been like her kid sister who'd always been the exciting one. Martine was "old reliable"—dependable, steadfast, sane, and the first line of defense between her father's acid tongue and her two younger siblings' feelings.

When I first met Martine, she had just had her heart broken by "the perfect man." A lawyer, he enjoyed showing off his beautiful girlfriend in public while privately running a steady and watchful eye over each morsel of food she ate and each piece of clothing she wore. Finally, she'd been dumped for another newer version of herself, one presumably with a better wardrobe and a more acceptable diet. Nonetheless, when she described the affair, she laid the burden of its demise squarely on herself—if she'd only dressed better, taken better care of herself, understood how important it was to him, she would now be the "Mrs." to his "Mr." Martine's self-confidence had taken such a beating that she'd fallen into a real depression and had begun psychotherapy.

"I can't believe it," she said, sounding completely exasperated. "Steve's just like the rest of them. Either that, or he's right—I *am* boring. What have we been doing here all this time?" she asked, turning to me testily. "All these hours, for what? I just keep ending up in the same place over and over again. I'm sick of it."

"Now we're getting somewhere," I thought.

Here's some good news: Most of our stories come with expiration dates. It's as though our personalities, having been built on these unstable fictions, finally collapse under the weight of all that twisting and compensating. We get so contorted trying to be all the things we think will get us love, connection, and intimacy, that everything just collapses under its own weight. We become overwhelmed by our baroque contortions and we break out in anxiety, dissatisfaction, dysfunction, depression—the emotional hit parade of miseries.

No change happens without these painful feelings. What would motivate us or make us willing to do the work required if we were comfortable and our lives were working well? Pain is the sign that our stories have stopped working. Instead of protecting us, their messages now block us from getting what we want or are causing us to lose something we treasure. We find that elements of our personalities have turned into liabilities or our defenses start to sound hollow—even to our own ears. When this happens, we experience an array of unpleasant emotions—all of which represent an opportunity to stop living unconsciously and start understanding our inner selves.

Some pretty honest and hard work lies ahead, but the bumps in the road are worth the ride. This is the point where many popular self-help methods try shortcuts in an attempt to get around the unconscious. Unfortunately, as promising and seductive as some of those paths may appear, in the end, they can't get us where we want to go. There's just no road to real without going through the valleys of the story and what lies beneath our conscious minds. As Ralph Waldo Emerson put it: "The best way out is through."

Remember the story of the velveteen rabbit and how he became real? His journey involved being separated from the boy who loved him, getting thown away, sitting in a garbage heap, being rained on, and enduring the painful powerlessness of not having any legs to run around with as the real rabbits had. Ultimately, however, going through that process made him real. At the end of the tale, he was loved for who he was. The same holds true here.

The process of becoming real begins when we stop tying our personalities up in neat bundles, presenting only what we think people want to see. And we will only become willing to do this when we're in so much pain emotionally that we have no alternative. But we don't—we can't—just turn on a dime. Prepare for a cyclical journey—one where, when you're open, you will see your behavior clearly, and when you're defended, you will wonder why on earth you thought anything was wrong with you or that you needed to change.

Signs That Your Story Has Stopped Working

To do the work of throwing off our storied personalities and becoming real, we have to be suffering enough to be motivated. Sorry. I wish it were otherwise. But as my car mechanic told me the other day, "Lady, I didn't build this thing, I only fix them." If you are in enough pain, you're going to commit the time and the patience to the process of change. If you do commit, you will have to withstand some frustrations, anxieties, and strong feelings, and you're going to do so without acting out in some defensive or self-destructive manner. The most natural response to emotional discomfort is to try to get rid of the feelings as quickly as possible. Try to tell yourself as you experience the anxiety that comes with the package that, without this feeling, no change is possible.

Here are the most common signs that your story has stopped working:

- Usual patterns of behavior start creating undesired results.
- You experience extremely painful emotions and have an inability to withstand them.

- You can't appreciate the good things in your life.
- You can't function at work, at home, or in your community.
- Your relationships become embattled.
- You're beaten down by chronic low moods or fear and anxiety.
- There's an external loss or crisis you can't absorb or respond to.
- Your anger becomes uncontrollable.
- Your body has mysterious breakdowns that your doctors can't explain medically.
- It slowly dawns on you that you've been really unfulfilled, unhappy, or anxious for years.

Instead of associating these things with a failure of will or character, try to see them for what they are—symptoms that you are outgrowing your old coping skills. A natural and very healthy breakdown is occurring with each one of these that is making space for a more authentic life.

Repetitive Behavior

Perhaps the most common sign that your story needs to be abandoned and rewritten is when you become aware—as Martine did—that you've been doing the same thing over and over again and it isn't doing what you wanted it to.

Most of us have learned to view repetitive behavior as proof that we are failures because, no matter how hard we seem to be trying, we end up learning the same old lesson over and over again. But we aren't flunking life. We aren't hopeless or inadequate or any of the other things we may feel at this moment. What we are is stuck. And we will continue to stay stuck until we become conscious that our same old behavior and choices are no longer giving us the results we desire.

Our personalities have a strange mechanism built into them—one that compels us to re-create the painful disappointments and conflicts of childhood. It's part of our basic human nature. Until we make the unconscious part of our characters visible, we will continue to respond to life as we did as children—holding on to love or support at the cost of our now-adult selves. It doesn't matter if it's a work or love situation. Whatever way our personality developed, it will keep acting out the same dramas until we intercede as adults, recognize that an old story scripts our experiences, and rewrite the tale.

These stories may have started in childhood, but as we've grown and changed, we've dressed them up, disguised them, updated them, and taken them on the road. The specifics may be different, the dramas acted out by different characters, but the central conflicts remain the same. The little kid who authored the story in the first place—usually for good reasons—still sits in the middle trying to resolve a painful situation between herself and someone she loves and needs.

When we're unaware of our patterns, we're like heat-seeking missiles—we are drawn to repeat the painful dilemmas of our past. We do this for a few reasons—the first is that we're attracted to what we know. It's comfortable. Life feels familiar. We get to use the skills that we developed that became part of our personalities. Because we are already living life according to our stories, we are unconsciously attracted to the people, places, and things that best suit their narratives.

The second reason we re-create patterns is that it is the mind's way of reprocessing trauma. It doesn't matter what the traumatic event was—it may have been one that would not appear at all earthshaking to anyone else. But the way the mind deals with deep upset is to replay it continually, gradually decreasing the threshold of the drama.

The third reason is the simplest. When we repeat behavior, we think it will do what it did for us as kids—allow us to hold on to what we love. That may seem counterintuitive, but think about it this way:

Fast forward. You're no longer a child but are now out in the dating world like Martine. Because you're compelled to repeat the trauma, you find yourself continually dating men who put you down or act superior. But you know how to swallow your upset and not show that you're hurt because as a kid, in order to have your father's approval, you learned not to say anything. You probably feel a little bit proud of the fact you can do that and not annoy your already trigger-happy beau with more emotionality. After all, you are too sensitive—and he's a strong, opinionated man. In fact, he will probably think highly of you because you can take his tough criticism, some of which—you admit to yourself—perhaps might be justified.

See how your story twists things? You absorb other people's not-so-nice behavior into your personality. You took some unpleasant behavior and unconsciously put it through the black box of your story, and it translated your boyfriend's really rather obnoxious behavior into something more acceptable. You will continue to have your reality obscured by your story as long as you repeat this pattern. You need the pattern to break down because, like all of us, you confuse your comfort with the familiar sense that maybe that's just the way life is. Maybe you think your love can change him. Or maybe you think you're the only one who understands him. There are countless variations of the story, all of which keep you from seeing the truth: Maybe you are doing something to invite this cruel behavior, or maybe this guy you're dating is just a jerk.

When you're stuck in repetitive patterns, you also can't see the entirety of your situation. Let's say that the man you're dating makes some honest comments to you that are appropriately communicative and intimate but include both good and bad things. All you can hear are the bad things because that's what you are used to and that's what your story tells you must be going on. You can't hear any of the good things because your pattern directs you away from them, and the bad things are amplified. So you think you're dating a critical guy like the rest of them, but what's really happened is that you've had selective hearing. That's often what goes on—it's not necessarily that you've got a broken relationship picker—it's that *all* men seem critical to you.

Remember that you were young and helpless when you started this behavior. In order to satisfy your primary need to be loved and protected, you had to make the world right, which has the destructive corollary of making you wrong. So what happens? Instead of seeing things for what they are, the message you send yourself is that these guys you're dating aren't nice to you, not because they are arrogant jerks but because *you* aren't good enough. If you were better, these guys (and your father) would treat you better because they really are great guys. By holding on to these guys at any price—usually your self-esteem—you hold on to the only source of love and approval you have ever known.

It's hard to believe that we set up these repetitive situations, but we do. We think it's an impulse—buying the new shoes, having the drink, ignoring our mates while we make sure the kitchen is spotless—but these patterns go far beyond simple tics or behaviors. Whenever we set up a situation that causes a problem that solves the original conflict (the one where our primary need was unfulfilled), we can step into an accustomed solution. What we do is reenact our hurts over and over again by dressing them up in different situations. Over time, we actually start re-creating the problems so that we can soothe ourselves with the comfortable resolutions. Thus, we continue to buy clothes that are too sexy for a specific occasion because we know we will get men's attention. Or maybe we don't stick up for ourselves when we deserve some recognition for hard work done. Or perhaps we date the same lout over and over again. Over time, such patterns of behavior become second nature. Before we are willing to go back to that first nature, though, these patterns have to stop producing the results we really want. Then, and only then, will we become willing to abandon them.

Ultimately, nothing will change until we learn to spot these old desires, now morphed into our patterns of behavior and guarded from view by our trusty defenses. Until we learn to look for these repetitions, they will continue to be the silent navigators of our days. They will continue to direct us exactly where we don't want to go. The task is to learn to "out" these stealth compasses so we can chart another, freer course for our lives.

Unbearable Emotions

Besides being sick and tired of repeated patterns, there are a number of other paths that lead to the turning point as well. Some emotions are so painful that we become willing to do whatever it takes to change whatever it is that is making us so unhappy. Experiences of profound fear, shame, guilt, anxiety, rage, grief, and loss all catapult people into seeking help. These emotions are acute and dramatic and can cut through all the normal defensive tactics that rise up when we contemplate changing the things that cause us pain. When we experience deep anguish, we become willing to look at our personalities in a new light. Especially if we're so miserable, we feel unable to bear standing in our own shoes another minute. This collapse represents a marvelous—if torturous—moment since it leads us right to the willingness to examine what has been off-limits.

Stuart had been a heavy drinker. One night during an alcoholic blackout, he had hit his teenage daughter, Alexandra, so hard that it broke her nose and she had to be taken to the hospital. He woke up with blood on his shirt but had no idea what had happened until someone told him. Too ashamed to ever speak of what happened to his family, he went to AA shortly after this horrible incident and had been sober for close to fifteen years. But now, with his daughter's wedding so close, he has fallen into a profound depression that alternates with outbreaks of rage. At work, when crossed or questioned, he has been erupting like a volcano. Each new day is worse than the last. He has also been arguing constantly with his wife, Susan, about the cost of the wedding, the food, the wine, about life itself, until she became so fed up that she told him that as soon as Alex was married, she was leaving him.

That crisis landed Stuart in my office, but it was his internal emotional state—more than his immediate marital crisis—that reverberated most profoundly. It didn't take long for us to see that with Alex's wedding coming up, sleeping dogs were rousing themselves from their beds. Although Alex had asked her father to walk her down the aisle, Stuart still felt tremendous guilt about what he had done to her years before. That guilt led him to the willingness to examine his own story about his life. Maybe he wasn't the victim he thought he was—of alcoholism, of his marriage, of his own drunken and raging father. Maybe he wasn't the guy everyone could depend on, which, after years in AA, is how he saw himself. Even with all the self-examination required by the AA program, his story remained hidden away, and not just to himself. It took an outer collapse to bring him to the point of looking at his inner one. He became ready to change whatever he needed to in order to get on with his life and make amends to his daughter, who he dearly loved, and save his marriage.

Grief

Grief, too, brings people to a state of readiness. Gretchen found herself suicidally depressed as she approached her thirty-third birthday. Extremely bright, successful, and charming, she was at a total loss to explain what was causing this truly debilitating crisis. Gretchen was a true Dependent—she gauged the value of her life by how she was or wasn't helping others. Now, having finished her residency in pediatrics, she couldn't get out of bed.

Through her personality, Gretchen had managed not to look at her story. Her mother had died when she was five, at the age of . . . thirty-three. Sometimes it doesn't take much detective work to see at what point the story intrudes in our lives. But even though Gretchen knew that much of what she did was motivated by her desire to give the world what she never got, she never guessed that this identification was holding her back from an authentic life. In fact, she thought it inspired it. It took coming up to the same age her mother was when she died to shake Gretchen into the conscious awareness that she had chosen to be a pediatrician as a sublimation of her fears that she had somehow been responsible for her mother's death. She had to have been responsible, right? Otherwise, why would her mother have died? Her mother was a good person and would never have left a five-year-old. In the twisted world of the story, this logic made perfect sense since it preserved Gretchen's mother as a loving figure. At the time her mother died from a protracted illness, Gretchen had been very angry with her mother for what she felt was an increasing abandonment as she got sicker and sicker. Ultimately, when her mother died, Gretchen felt that her own anger had killed her mother. She became a doctor to try to deal with her unconscious feelings of being so lethal, but her profession had ultimately failed to shield her.

Compounding her situation, Gretchen began to feel bad about her childlessness. But what she began to realize as she faced her grief was that she hadn't wanted kids because she was afraid they might do to her what she feared she had done to her own mother. Thus, her mourning her mother became wrapped up with her own fear of mortality—children equaled death in her unconscious story.

Depression

Gretchen's profound and unprocessed grief created a depression. At this juncture, her depression may have been biological as well as psychological, but it was the symptom that her story had stopped working for her. Depression—that feeling of tremendous sadness—can relate to something tangibly external like losing a loved one, a job, a dream. Or it can come from a perceived loss—loss of youth, loss of parental love. Depression naturally occurs even though we have come to look at it as something to be universally avoided. As kids grow up, they go through periods of depressed moods as they pass from one stage of dependence to another and ultimately to independence. Depression also serves a purpose for adults. As in Gretchen's case, it stopped her from living unconsciously and created a roadblock that shook her from her story. In order to get through her sadness, she has to make a decision to recognize her story and stop letting it hold her back. Her depression is telling her she must address some things she's avoided and reevaluate her life.

Shame and Guilt

Shame and guilt are two other painful emotions that shake people from their stories. Shame is a feeling of humiliation, and it differs from guilt, which is more of a feeling that you've done something wrong. Guilt is a natural response to a conflict in your value system—like cheating on someone. Shame is something else—it's a feeling that something about you is just wrong, humiliating, or embarrassing. These emotional cousins are found in all the personality types.

Shame doesn't care what your actions are—you're just plain old wrong as a human being. Roger, a compulsive womanizer and a Self-defeater, never got over the fact that he arrived only four months after his parents got married. His parents had really hated each other throughout his childhood, and because he couldn't hate them, he hated himself as the cause of their unhappiness. His self-loathing became so bad that he needed to prove to himself that he was evil incarnate— something he did by having sex with women and not telling them he carried the sexually transmitted disease herpes. He created a situation that mirrored his inner shame until finally he could no longer live with his actions and was forced to own up to them and change.

Guilt can be equally corrosive. Andi had put her whole life on hold when her mother became terminally ill. She did everything for her in ways that amazed people. It looked for all the world like Andi was a devoted daughter, but these visits came not from love but from guilt that she couldn't take away her mother's Alzheimer's disease.

But Andi's guilt backfired. She lost her job because caring for her mother took so much time. She jeopardized her living situation and cut herself off from her social life, all because, Dependent that she is, she felt so guilty about not being a good enough daughter to this woman who had been so distant to Andi as a child. Her mother was an extremely self-absorbed person who had never really wanted children. This created such anger in Andi that she had a lot of very negative feelings about her mother, which caused her to feel guilty. Andi landed in my office because as she tried to make up for these feelings of guilt, she began to destroy herself.

Rage

Andi's brother, Nate, however, reacted to his mother's illness with rage. He couldn't direct his uncontrolled fury. "She never did a thing for me," he yelled at his sister when she asked for his help. "Why should I lift a finger for her?" He was a Self-defeater, so his expression differed totally from Andi's even though the emotions sprung from the same source. At work, his boss had to have a conversation with him about how cruel he was being to the support staff. One more outburst and they'd be risking a harassment lawsuit, his boss said. He ordered Nate to take two weeks off, which only meant that he brought his anger home. His kids completely avoided him. And his wife, sick of being the object of his repeated accusations and beatings, told him that if he didn't cut it out, she was going to ask him to move out. When he put a nasty dent in his car trying to swing around a slow-moving car and smashed the front end into a fire hydrant, Nate's wife sought help for him. She loved him and knew that watching his mother die was horrible for him, but she knew she was not about to become the object of his rage.

We're more accustomed to seeing angry men than women in our society. Women also experience the pain of overwhelming anger, but women generally also have more trouble expressing and living with it. I see so many women who feel utterly ashamed of themselves for screaming at their children or slapping them in moments when their fury causes them to lose control. Or they shut down and sink deeply into depression as they block the expression but not the source of the anger. The internal conflict hurts so much, however, that they're in a great position to be motivated to discover the anger's source.

External Crisis

Many people finally become willing to address their stories when an external crisis forces them to stop their "business as usual" ways. Maggie's moment came when she answered the door and found a sobbing woman with an infant. It was the wife of the man Maggie had been having an affair with, a woman she had vilified in her mind to justify her own behavior. Whether or not this miserable woman was an angel or a devil, it didn't matter. Maggie saw that her passions were harming real people. Confronted with the consequences of her action, Maggie's story crumbled.

So did Diane's—when her husband turned to her and said he was leaving her because she wouldn't lose the fifty pounds that was harming her health and that had killed their sex life. A Dependent who'd been expecting him to leave her for years, Diane had packed the pounds on in preparation. Turns out they created her worst nightmare. When forced to see how she had created the fulfillment of her worst fears, Diane realized that if she had the power to create the problem, she might just have the power to fix it.

Our Bodies Fail Us

One of the personality traits of Dependents is that they can't ask for help unless they fall apart physically. But somatic (of the body) episodes are not confined to them. High blood pressure, fatigue, and migraines are just some of the signs that our stories can no longer explain and absorb the conflicts in our lives.

I've had patients with chronic headaches, backaches, and stomach pains who go to doctors who tell them, "reduce your stress"—like anyone has a clue what to do with that! Here they are, type As, and then the physician tells them to try to take a few things out of their lives that they think will reduce the stress level. What happens is almost the opposite. Now they have *more* time to be anxious, depressed, angry, or fearful about whatever actually was going on internally in the first place because there are fewer distractions.

Chronic Unhappiness

Then there's the final group, one in which I would place Leslie. Leslie had been down so long, she'd come to accept it as her biological makeup. She'd been to doctors but each sent her away with an antacid, a prescription for a mild tranquilizer, and some generic advice about stress reduction.

Leslie felt no excitement in her life, just the grind of everyday life. She had a job that was okay. An apartment that was okay. A boyfriend she liked but didn't feel great passion for. At thirty-two, she felt she'd slowed down on her career path, and nothing got her terribly excited. Leslie, in truth, felt terribly unfulfilled—like everything was only half of what it should be. Chronically disappointed in herself, her work, and her friends, Leslie felt that the joy had slipped away.

These are people who, like Leslie, feel beaten down by chronic low moods or fear or anxiety. They are deflated or depressed. Some are so debilitated by these feelings that they have stopped functioning. With others, these feelings boil away at a slow simmer.

The people in this slow-simmer group become willing to examine their stories because it has slowly dawned on them that they've been unhappy or anxious *for years*. They stand back from their lives and see that they are never going to get where they want to go. They don't enjoy their marriages the way they want to or find the mates they desire. They aren't being the kind of parents they want to be. These people feel blocked in their lives and ground down by circumstances. Most have explored other avenues to feeling better—exercise, workshops, even medication—but ultimately end up feeling utterly defeated by any attempt to change.

We have all had the experience of feeling we are making progress only to relapse. Dieters yo-yo, and daters serially date the "wrong" guys. Drinkers pick up drinks, and drug users try just a little now that they've "gotten a handle" on their habits. Spenders splurge on that must-have item. We swear off self-destructive behaviors, we seek cures, we read books, we get help, but for most of us, we end up back at square one too often. Sometimes, we're just visiting, and we quickly pick ourselves up and move on. But whether we are stuck back where we started from or not, we all know the feeling that we have deeply let ourselves down. But when we start looking at the feeling of being overwhelmed by our lives as a promising starting point instead of the end of a downward spiral, we can start to see that these awful feelings are signposts and not destinations. They can direct us out of our stories and into our real selves.

The Value of Pain

The silver lining in all these experiences is that they produce so much discomfort that our old personalities and defenses aren't equipped to make the pain go away. We have to try new ways, develop new coping mechanisms, rewrite old stories. Thus, emotional pain becomes the catalyst for all change. When the stories we created to protect ourselves instead promise misery or create the situations we most fear, it sets up a conflict so great that our stories themselves stop working. For many people it takes these kinds of dramatic confrontations for them to become willing to do the necessary work.

Chapter Six

TURNING PAIN INTO PROGRESS

By now, you know your personality type—Dependent, Super-achiever, Perfectionist, Self-defeater, or Competitor—so you can begin to look for the characteristic behaviors and automatic reactions. The truth is that no matter how miserable you are, no matter how your story overwhelms you, no matter how much your personality starts getting in the way of your happiness, unless you make a conscious decision to actively turn your emotional pain into progress, nothing will happen. It is this pain that will lead you to the awareness of your particular story. Because you know your personality type, you can spot the unconscious reactions that used to control you when your personality type's story takes over. This is where the pain part comes in—pain is what brings the unconscious to our awareness. Think about outgrowing an old pair of shoes. If you don't get a larger size, you'll get blisters on your feet. Something will rub you the wrong way and you'll have to change your shoes. Well, psychic and emotional pain works the same way: It asks you to become aware of what in your story has been rubbing you the wrong way. The only way to relieve the pain is to remove the constricting story and replace it with one that fits better. But we can do this only by becoming aware of what it is that is causing us to hurt. When we find that out, we uncover our stories.

This chapter outlines three powerful tools that, when practiced, will lead you to your particular story:

1. *Sit, don't act.* This allows you to locate your biggest conflicts and emotional pain without your story's causing you to automatically act out.
2. *Shift from victim to storyteller.* Changing your perspective on your life and current conflicts removes the powerlessness that underlies all stories.
3. *Look, don't judge.* When we treat ourselves with empathy and compassion, we can revisit the original stories as mature adults and see how to rewrite them.

Prioritize Your Mind

Up to now, we've been talking about the unconscious and how it directs us without our awareness or permission. Now we get to use our conscious minds in order to take our lives off the automatic pilot. Before we use these powerful tools, we have to prioritize our minds—we have to decide that the most important thing we can do is change our mental and emotional shoes.

Big deal, you say. Make a decision. Sure. Like deciding to lose those last ten pounds or to have sex more often with our spouses. Just like that. Well, nobody said this was easy. But without the active decision to begin the process of change, without the decision to stop and look and try to understand, we will remain stuck in the same patterns unreleased from the pain that has haunted us for our entire lives.

What is this decision? It's a choice we make to prioritize our minds. I've had patients with all the money in the world, the greatest jobs, the most wonderful spouses, the most accomplished children. But their lives were miserable because their stories had stopped working. So, like them, if we don't decide we're going to make it our first priority to take the time and effort to uncover our stories and free ourselves from their rules, we can have all the external goodies in the world but no way to enjoy them.

Prioritizing our minds means thinking about what makes us anxious before we act to discharge that anxiety through automatic and unconscious behaviors. When we don't get invited to the "in" party, when our spouses forget our anniversaries, when our children forget about Mother's Day and Father's Day, when a friend makes an innocent comment about our visible panty lines or wrinkles, all of these can call up the old stories about how inadequate or forgotten we feel. When that happens, we respond without thinking from the old wounded places by setting up familiar dynamics. Dependents will find ways to shift the focus to others and avoid intimacy; Self-defeaters will become so passive that those around them become infuritated. We retreat into old patterns and old behaviors.

You can tell right away when you find yourself in any of these self-made (but unconscious) situations—you'll find you're repeating unwanted behaviors, feeling outbreaks of depression, having a larger emotional response to a situation than it calls for, or any of the signs that our stories have stopped working. Once you realize that finding yourself back where you started is not bad fortune but a symptom that your story is breaking down, then you can step outside its narrow boundaries and become aware both of it and the decisions it's making for you.

Prioritizing our minds means that we'll learn to stop before we responsively act out old scenarios. It means stepping out of the action and asking ourselves, "What am I about to do here? Why do I want to do this?" These quick questions act as a manual override to the automatic system and can short-circuit the story's programming.

These questions are no guarantee that we still won't say something catty about the hostess of the party or give our spouses or children the silent treatment because we're not yet aware of our unconscious instructions. But stopping before acting will open the door to that awareness even as it reinforces that we have a choice in all our reactions. When we see that we can make decisions at every step of the way, we begin to regain some control in our lives.

Quite often, people come into my office and say something like, "Okay, you've just told me I'm a Perfectionist and, okay, that's true, I accept it. But what can I *do*?" They want a three-step answer. But instead, I tell them that we can't immediately cough out a process. What needs to happen first of all is that they must sit quietly and commit to making different choices when they find themselves in familiar situations. Instead of turning on the TV at night, I tell them they're going to have to sit and think about what's troubling them and try to become conscious of their actions and automatic reactions.

"But it's *not* a choice!" I hear all the time when I am examining someone's behavior. "It happened so fast I couldn't stop myself!" Well, you probably won't be able to stop yourself at first. Making a decision doesn't mean not acting. Sometimes it means you've got the insight but it's still hard to interrupt years of defensive programming.

In the beginning of this process, we can get discouraged when we stop, think, and still do the precise thing we didn't want to do. But that is why we need to make the decision a priority. If we don't, we will give up at our first failure and fall back into the denial, the projection, and the other defenses that have kept us sealed in.

The Goal Is Awareness

A few years ago I did a segment for the *Today* show on New Year's resolutions. I told the viewers that one of the most important resolutions they could possibly make for the new year was to look for patterns in their lives. Awareness of these patterns, I told them, would lead them to amazing self-discoveries.

Well, I've had big responses before, but nothing like this. Beginning that same day, a flood of calls swamped my answering machine. "Every time a relationship gets good, it blows up." "As soon as people tell me I look great, I eat it all back on." "It happens over and over; I get close to a promotion and then I blow it." The examples came from every area of people's lives.

I was shocked by how little it took to get such a huge reaction. Maybe I shouldn't have been so surprised, since finding ourselves trapped in unwanted behavior patterns frustrates us more than almost anything else. But the response spoke volumes to me about how easy it is, when we're ready, to be aware.

That's the really good news. No matter what your personality type, no matter what your defenses, no matter which pattern you continue to repeat, when you become aware of your repetitive behaviors, you've taken the first step to becoming free of the past.

The reason we need to be aware of our patterns of behavior is simple and powerful—exposing them makes what we are protecting visible. Until we do that, our defenses, our patterns, our reactions remain in the unconscious, hidden away from our understanding and thus our control. Once we make them conscious, we will have the choice to stop using them. We will be able to stop re-creating unwanted situations. We will peel off the layers that stand between us and being real.

This is the goal—to bring to our adult consciousness the awareness of when the child's hidden story is calling the shots in our lives. But awareness needs fertile soil in order to seed and grow. This is where the three important tools mentioned before—(1) sit, don't act; (2) shift from victim to storyteller; and (3) look, don't judge—will help you become aware of your story.

Tool 1. Sit, Don't Act

Awareness is great. There's just one big problem with it, though. It can make us so anxious that we are willing to do *anything*—spend, eat, drink, lie, run out—not to have to sit through the feelings. Anxiety acts as the starting gun at the opening gate of the old behaviors that we developed precisely to soothe our original anxieties about not being lovable, acceptable, or adequate. So my first advice while we're going through this process is to not act out on any urgent feelings. This tool was very important for Sunny, a Dependent with many Self-defeater qualities. When I met her, she was in the process of divorcing but was so terrified of her soon-to-be ex-husband that she couldn't negotiate her settlement well. They were at the two sticking points—child visitation (Sunny didn't want it unsupervised) and child support (he was using the threat of no money if she didn't let him have the kids alone).

But Sunny's husband was a bully who had hit their children. Sunny knew all too well the kind of terror that created—she, too, had been the child of an abusive father who alternated between hitting her and ignoring her completely. The story that came out of it was "If I'm a doormat, then they'll like me," and she developed the kind of personality that didn't rile people up. But that story wasn't going to work, and every time she tried to depart from its instructions, she became overwhelmed with anxiety, ready to give away the store just to quell the feelings. But this set up a crisis for Sunny—expose the kids or expose her story. She couldn't safeguard them and make her anxiety go away. She was going to have to sit through the feelings without acting on them this time. There was no way she could be the people pleaser she was without exposing her children to more of her husband's abuse or face financial penalties, and Sunny did not want her children's lives hurt or compromised.

I told Sunny that she was going to have to stop and think before she acted during the negotiations of her divorce settlement. Her personality would automatically capitulate to her ex—her default position would be to avoid his anger by trading just about anything for a peaceful connection to him. But this time, even she could see that if she did that, she'd be having her children pay for her story. She was going to have to change how she saw herself and what her story told her to do in order to do the best thing for her children and herself.

Anxiety almost crippled Sunny as she contemplated the coming negotiations without the comfort of her familiar survival skills and well-honed defenses. But because she sat through the feelings, she could see the consequences of her pattern of placating others at her own expense. She made the decision not to do that here because she couldn't hurt her children. By going through the negotiations fully aware of her compensatory personality, she not only made a better settlement agreement but also discovered something vital about herself. She realized she was perfectly able to survive and thrive on her own. She wasn't a powerless child anymore. She could give up caving in to everyone all the time. In fact, she was beginning to see that she didn't ever again need to give in to anyone in order to be loved. Sunny was able to reach in and pull out some of that true independence inside her—the independence that had led her to protect her children. She was able to see that the old Sunny had gotten into this mess and the real Sunny would get her out.

As we arrive at this point, it is important to remember that *when we began relying on our stories and built our personalities around them to soothe our anxieties, we also preserved the original emotions we were feeling in their unadulterated, childhood forms.* That means that as we become conscious of our characters, we will have to return to the emotions of our childhood—to the hurt, the fear, and the disappointment that caused us to create our stories in the first place. Sunny reexperienced a real terror of abuse and abandonment during the divorce—not only by her husband but also by her father. Her anxiety about not acting the way she normally would have in the past made perfect sense. Inside, she was still a little kid trying to find a way to get love from her father. However, once Sunny saw her story in the light of the current day, it no longer held the same power and ability to produce anxiety for her.

I cannot say enough how powerful and tender a place this is. I know people who have refused to examine themselves because they didn't want to risk going back and seeing the good, the bad, and the ugly about the father they've idolized or the mother they've adored or the sibling they've defended. They also didn't want to see what they contributed to their own suffering. At our cores, we are still emotionally the little kids whose primary needs were frustrated. We are still holding on to that love and recognition we crave, even at the cost of the unreal life.

When we're anxious, sitting without acting is one of the hardest tasks imaginable. Inside, most of us feel this anxiety with all the urgency of a life-or-death situation. We want to do something and do it quickly. But once we start the old behaviors in motion, it's like a cigarette smoker inhaling that nicotine after a few hours' withdrawal. The anxiety ebbs, and we automatically do what needs to be done—whatever it is we've always done—to get through a circumstance without getting close to the source of what set up the problem in the first place.

Locate the Biggest Conflict in Your Life

The best way to begin the practice of awareness is to stop reading for a minute and locate the biggest problem in your life today. As with Sunny, you will find that it is shrouded with anxiety, you won't want to look at it, and you'll become overwhelmed suddenly with the urge to scrub the inside of your refrigerator or clean your hubcaps. But remember—sit, don't act.

It may sound simple, but it's not easy. The only way to change is to interrupt the automatic nature of our lives. Then—and only then—do we have a fighting chance with the unconscious.

Where there's smoke there's fire. If you want to know what your story is, here's a great starting point. Think about it. Where do you feel angry, ashamed, hurt, or abandoned? Is it with your mate? Your sibling? A former best friend? A boss?

When I asked Caroline to locate the biggest conflict in her life, it was a no-brainer. At thirty-five, Caroline was a star. She was the mother of two and the most successful analyst in her investment bank, with a nice record of accomplishment behind her at other companies. She had moved around from company to company—she'd never liked her bosses, and moving seemed the only way she'd ever get a decent raise. But lately, she'd been pretty happy with her position.

That is until Lawrence became her new boss. Caroline couldn't get over having another awful boss. She thought she'd left the last one behind five years ago. And this time, it was her own fault. The vice president of her division had asked her if she wanted to become the regional manager of her bank. Caroline had just had her second child, however, and felt that she'd be too overwhelmed if she took on a job that involved a lot more travel. Instead, she recommended her coworker, Lawrence, a young man with no family commitments. She had always respected him and thought that she would enjoy working with him. She also hoped—although she didn't articulate this to herself at the time—that he'd be open to her need for a flexible schedule and that he'd welcome suggestions and advice since she had seniority. A win-win situation, she thought.

It hadn't taken long for friction to develop. At first, it centered on her unusual work arrangement. As a risk analyst, Caroline didn't need to have client contact. When Lawrence took over, she continued with her prior arrangement to work at home a couple of afternoons a week so she could be near her kids. The main office began pressuring

Lawrence about Caroline's schedule, and he asked her to report her afternoons at home as absences. This didn't sit well with her, and she began a pattern of passive aggression with her boss that culminated in a nasty standoff between the two former friends.

The conflict began consuming her. She felt betrayed. After all, he wouldn't even have this job if she hadn't suggested him. Lawrence's demands for increased accountability—not just in her hours but in how she developed her reports—infuriated her. Didn't she have much more experience than he? Wasn't she more respected in her industry?

Soon, the conflict spilled out into public with the two of them snapping at each other in meetings and through E-mails with others copied on them as unfortunate witnesses. Caroline felt isolated and vulnerable at work and exhausted at home because she couldn't sleep. Every night between two and four in the morning, she had lengthy imaginary mental discussions with Lawrence, telling him exactly what she felt he needed to hear. She wanted him to shut up and leave her alone, and she was filled with rage over his nervy disrespect.

Caroline is acting out something very primal in her life. She is creating a situation that brings up the same feelings of not having her needs met—those primary ones that were frustrated in her earliest years. The only way she is ever going to become aware of this, though, is if she can sit in her current conflict and feel all the feelings her actions are trying to assuage.

I asked Caroline if she had the guts to sit through her rage and her anxiety. Because if she could do that, she would find she'd soon hit the mother lode and when she did so, I promised her that she'd never again lose sleep over a bad boss.

I asked Caroline to describe both her automatic actions and how she felt about her conflict with Lawrence. This is what she came up with:

1. I withhold information from him because I resent his intrusion.
2. I tell others that I could have had that job so they know I'm superior.
3. I'm so angry with him I wish he would fail and fail publicly.
4. I gossip about him behind his back.
5. I feel unfairly picked on because he's threatened by me.

This was a pretty good and honest list. I then asked Caroline to look for other relationships in her life—past or present—where any one of these feelings or actions existed. Remember that your story repeats itself in patterns; it will dress up in other guises, but your feelings and reactions will be the same. Your story will cause you to re-create in other times and places the exact dynamic that most plagues you at the moment. For Caroline, it showed up in two places.

The first was with her sister. For years, the two girls had had a thorny relationship. Susan had taken it on herself to act every inch of the big sister role with Caroline, up to and including being Caroline's critical police guard with boyfriends, school, weight, and appearance. Susan equated her love for her sister with a stream of suggestions, advice, and commentary, all of which was unwanted by the younger sister. Just last week, in fact, Susan had discovered that Caroline hadn't told her that the baby had scarlet fever, and Caroline was paying for her omission with a lengthy guilt trip delivered telephonically just as Caroline was trying to finish up a report for Lawrence. Now that she thought about it, Caroline saw that her relationship with her sister felt similar to her relationship with Lawrence. And her behavior felt familiar as well.

The other thing Caroline came up with was the fact that each of her jobs spanning back thirteen years had ended badly with her supervisor or boss. In each case, she had left feeling disrespected, unappreciated, and smarter than her superiors. Either she had a really bad nose for employers, I told her, or the pattern was the product of her story.

Like Caroline, every one of us has a central conflict that echoes down the corridors of other relationships and other situations. Our job is to look for the patterns in our lives where those conflicts are present.

Practicing the First Tool

Take a minute and close your eyes. Think about the fight you had with your boss, your mate, your sibling, yourself. Think about something you did that made you feel terrible about yourself. Look at situations during which your emotions run highest—that tells you that you have a story behind what is going on.

Tool 2. Shift from Victim to Storyteller

We have to remember that we created our stories in response to very real situations. Two feelings lie at the center of every story—powerlessness and the sense of being a victim. But the powerlessness must be exposed for what it is—a vestige. We can't do that if we remain unaware that we are still seeing life from this helpless and victimized perspective. Once we have sat through the emotions and seen how current situations reenact old stories, we can move to the next tool—empowering ourselves by switching from powerless to powerful, from child to adult, from victim to storyteller.

Virginia's real life story was pretty sad. Her mother was depressed most of her life. In an attempt to run the household in his wife's mental absence, Virginia's father became a tough drill sergeant who was highly critical and not afraid to "use his belt" if he had to. Most of his anger at his powerless wife fell on Virginia, the only girl of their five kids. Although she developed a brave front, Virginia blew up to close to 180 pounds by the time she was in high school. This left her a social outcast and the easy target of her father's rage. Because expressing any anger was too dangerous, Virginia turned the situation in on herself and developed the story that created a Self-defeater personality.

If you asked her if she felt sorry for herself, she'd tell you that she didn't. If you asked her if she was angry, the answer would be no, not really, that's just the way things were. But Virginia *was* angry. Furious, really. She felt she'd been robbed of her parents' love and any kind of social life at all. She'd met and married Jerry following a year and a half of Overeaters Anonymous. She'd never been thinner and never felt better about herself. But it wasn't going to last. Her first pregnancy brought an additional fifty pounds, her second another thirty. Jerry had long since pulled away sexually, leaving her depressed and enraged.

Did Virginia have a legitimate beef about her life? Absolutely. I would wager that almost everyone I see has reason to be unhappy and even dysfunctional. By definition, anyone who has developed a personality based on the hurts of childhood—that is to say *everybody*—has a reason to feel like a victim: powerless, abandoned, misunderstood, unappreciated.

The problem with being a victim, though, is that you will never break free of those feelings. If we look at the five main stories and personality types, we can see that being a victim is embedded in each one. These feelings come directly from the powerlessness of childhood when we couldn't defend ourselves or get our own needs met to be secure individuals, who are loved, attended to, and seen and appreciated for who we are. The resulting perspective that we carry within our personalities into adulthood, however, means we cling to a narrative that continues to cast us in the role of victims of circumstance.

Let's look briefly at the victim story line in each personality type. See if you can spot some of humanity's greatest hits in these victimized perspectives:

- *The Dependent* feels, "No one will ever love me the way I need to be loved. Therefore, I won't need anyone—I can do it myself. My needs are so great they overwhelm people and make them abandon me. I'm nothing without you, but if I let you into my heart, you will take me over and then leave me." These people tend to feel that everything is their own fault. Because they need people so much, they almost invite people to abandon them by their irritating and obsessive self-sufficiency.

- *The Superachiever* feels, "No one understands me. I have the potential for greatness. I have to be perfect or else no one will love me and I will be worthless." These people feel they are the victims of anyone who doesn't understand their true greatness. Even the slightest criticism sends these people spiraling down, because they feel that people just don't understand them.

- *The Self-defeater* feels, "I have to give myself up to be loved by you. I do everything for you and you still don't appreciate me. But you won't let me get angry or be critical or stand up for myself or you will leave me. I am always being controlled!" They believe they *have* to play the role of victim to be loved and accepted.

- *The Competitor* feels, "People only love me if I am pretty. I want to be loved for who I am, but no one does. If I compete, I will be hated, criticized, or rejected. But if I don't compete, I'll never get anyone to hold on to." This group usually feels the victim of people's envy, judgment, and exploitation. They're right. They just don't see, however, that they invite it through overly sexualized behavior or cutthroat competitiveness.

- *The Perfectionist* feels the world is against them. "What's wrong with this world? I'm at the mercy of people who have no idea how to do things right. I hate it when things are out of control. People should listen to me because I know how to make sure things get done correctly." They are the perpetual victims of people who don't understand how damaging big emotions and any disorder—emotional or otherwise—can be.

How, then, do we shift away from those feelings that come out of the powerlessness that sits at the core our personalities? We do it by switching our perspective. We remind ourselves that we are not powerless children anymore but capable adults. This is a huge shift. If we can start to see that we had a hand in creating our present circumstances, that we were not just the passive victims of our pasts but active agents in them, we can begin to have some control over what happens next.

How do we do this? In the case of Virginia, I asked her to tell me her story using only the first person "I." For example, she wasn't allowed to say that Jerry caused her recent weight gain; she had to keep the focus squarely on herself. I asked her to try to do this with as little judgment as possible. What I wanted Virginia to see was that she was powerful. She had created the very situation that made Jerry so upset and her so ashamed. She'd snuck into the refrigerator in the middle of the night, picked up the spoon, and dug into the vats of mint-chocolate-chip ice cream. She had set the stage so that she could retreat into her accustomed role of being seen as an unappealing person.

After a few attempts, her story changed. Jerry's disappointment didn't make her eat. She ate because she felt anxious and tired. The kids' squabbling didn't force her to pick up the spoon. Her own anger did—she would show them—she'd get fat again. Then they'd see how they were harming her. Instead of a fluid tale that ended in "I do everything for them and they don't appreciate me," Virginia saw that she was always going to construct a story that left her the victim. I promised her that as long as she ended up in that role, she would stay stuck right where she was—with a spoon in her hand and her head halfway into the refrigerator.

Virginia needs to do what Caroline did—see that her own actions contributed to her current conflict. Where Caroline gossiped, Virginia ate on the sly. Both resulted in re-creating their starring roles in the stories of their childhoods.

Use Your Fantasies to Expose Your Story

Take a moment and revisit your conflict. What is your role in it? Where have you felt like a victim? What made you feel that way? Can you think of anything you might have done or said to have contributed to the outcome? The imagination is such a powerful tool. Remember, when you put yourself in that conflict, do so without taking an action! Shift the focus from the other person's actions to yours. Remember what you are feeling right now. What is your fantasy about what you are going to do with that feeling? What do you feel your options are? The challenge now is to imagine a response to the feelings that arise in the conflict, because those reactions are designed to lead us away from our unconscious.

When I ask Sydney to do this, she immediately nods her head—the first thing that comes to mind is a fight she had last weekend with her fiancé, Brian. When he picked her up for dinner on Friday night, she was surprised to see two packed suitcases in the car. Brian had planned a romantic getaway at a country inn as a surprise. But Sydney hates surprises. She was irritated and snapped at him. "Forget it," Brian shot back. "I just can't win with you."

Sydney's first response to anything that involves either intimacy or loss of control will be negative. Her Dependent personality (with a heavy dose of Perfectionist) creates distance whenever possible—it's her way of protecting herself. If she isn't making the plans, she doesn't feel safe. If she's left alone with someone with no distractions, she feels anxious.

I asked Sydney to picture the moment and tell me what she felt.

"Fear," she answered. "I got overwhelmed with anxiety. And then I got mad. Yes, he made me so damned furious. It was so selfish of him. But it wasn't. But that's what got me crazy."

Her response didn't surprise me. Remembering that Sydney's father had gone out one day for a pack of cigarettes and never returned, I knew that Sydney could not tolerate feeling that she had no control over a situation that involved an intimate connection. Sydney couldn't handle emotional closeness because of her fears of losing Brian, so she unconsciously short-circuited the entire weekend.

Once she had located her biggest conflict, I asked her to shift from victim to storyteller and to rewrite the incident not focused on Brian's actions but on her own—real or imagined. In order to empower her, I wanted her to tell me all the fantasies she had about what would have made her feel better during that conflict. Did she want to tell Brian to take a hike? Did she imagine that no matter how poorly she treated him he'd always stick by her? I wanted her to be aware of the dramas that were running through her mind because they all point back to her need to have a man love her and stick by her.

Fantasizing about our choices allows us to put ourselves back in the story and rewrite it from an adult, empowered perspective. This is the key to switching out of victim mode. Remember, our unconscious story's first mission is to soothe anxiety and keep us from reexperiencing the pains of our original conflicts. So if we want to really get down to the deepest levels and see the story, we have to interpret the automatic behavior we have become programmed by over the years. Before our personalities and their action plans automatically kick in, we need to try and stay with those first emotions and engage our imaginations. Stop and ask these questions:

- What is your fantasy about your choices in the middle of your current conflict?
- What kinds of reactions do you imagine are possible?
- What dramas in your mind are being replayed?
- Who is included in these fantasies?

This may seem a little odd, but our fantasies are windows to our unconscious. They allow us to see what our real wishes and fears are in any given situation. The goal is to get to the point where we clearly see what the fantasy is—what we load onto the other person.

For Sydney, she imagines two scenarios—in the first, she is the victim and has no choice. If he is to stay with her, Brian must be obeyed. She must give herself up to him completely or he will leave her forever. She's been trying that one and it hasn't been working too well. She hates being out of control and that makes her irritable, so he's unhappy, too.

In Sydney's second scenario, she tells Brian exactly where he can shove his controlling plans. But as she plays that scene through, it ends the same way—with a relationship that is destined to fail, either because she has to disappear or because she makes him do the same. By looking at those two fantasies, Sydney can finally become conscious of her story—that intimacy equals abandonment. In the first fantasy, to hold on to love she must abandon herself, and in the second, being herself means she will be abandoned. It's a no-win victim-based story.

When we can become conscious of these fantasies, we see how we have been living according to the story's unconscious plotline. As adults, we are powerful. Each of us has the ability to create our choices—we can write different endings. But as long as we are governed by the unconscious, we won't have that option. Exposing our fantasies shows us the invisible plotline we will keep acting on if we don't stop and see that our actions are still being controlled by the emotions of the little children we were when our stories began. When we explore our fantasies, they expose our stories and allow us to witness the exact nature of our conflicts.

Until we bring our imagined scenarios to the surface, we will continue to act out our worst fears that will lead us precisely where we

don't want to go. By bringing the story's messages into our consciousness, we begin to see the price we've paid, how outdated our story is,
and how it has limited our repertoire of possibilities. We also begin to
see how we can change.

Betsey used this process in a particularly powerful way. Betsey, an
advertising executive, worked for Nancy, a maniac who was legendary
in her industry. This woman regularly yelled at people and humiliated
them in meetings. Betsey had a three-year-old and for the previous
year had been trying to get pregnant again. She came to see me because
her doctor told her that her job stress contributed to her trouble con-
ceiving.

Betsey knew that trying to mollify and defuse her boss was taking a
real toll on her. When I asked her to locate her biggest conflict, she
laughed. "That's easy, it's with Nancy. She's furious with me for all the
time I'm taking trying to get pregnant. She says if I keep this up, I'll
end up being fired." I asked her about her feelings, and Betsey admitted to feeling guilty, that indeed, she was "stealing" Nancy's time and
therefore causing the problems at work. In other words, Betsey had
done with Nancy what she had done with her own mother—shifted
the responsibility for her abusive behavior onto her own shoulders,
making herself the source of the problems and absolving both angry
women.

Betsey's fantasies about what she can and can't do in this situation
clearly show her story's conflict. She says she can either say "Nancy,
you are an abusive witch and you are destroying my health," which
will get her fired, or she can continue to do what she feels she's
doing—an excellent job both at work and at swallowing her stress.
Betsey doesn't have a choice; she needs the work (and, consequently,

she suffers the punishment of giving up her dreams of having another child—a perfect formula for a Self-defeater, a personality type that fits Betsey well).

Feeling powerless and trapped between a witch woman and the need for a job, Betsey became depressed and started to screw up at work. She began walking around thinking, "I'm such a screwup," instead of thinking, "This is my way of getting my wish to get fired because I can't stand working for this woman, but it wouldn't be right of me to quit."

"What do you want for yourself?" I ask Betsey. "Do you want to feel you can please the most unpleasable person? Will it make you an okay person if you do this? Is it your fantasy that you can succeed at a job no matter what the circumstances? Do you imagine you can change people?" I ask these things because if Nancy represents someone else to her then all those things will come into play. Her fantasy that she was doing her utmost best but that she has to succumb to a horror show of a boss was not true. The truth was that she was acting out in a much more indirect way. She began screwing up because she really wanted to get out of there. As long as she was unaware of her story—that she was going to be punished for being bad by her mean mother no matter what—she didn't have the option of looking at her situation and saying, "I really want to leave. Now let me examine my options."

Betsey believed this is the "one and only" job, the job she *must* have. She felt that her whole well-being depended on maintaining the connection. Well, that's the story at work. No one ever has a "one and only" job. People can always change jobs—it may not be that easy, it may take time and effort, but people who get stuck in a place where they feel this is the "one and only" have a story ruling their feelings that has a lot to do with a parental figure. When you are a kid, your parent is your "one and only." You have only one mother and father and you can't get new ones. You *can* get a new boss. But if you're stuck in a dynamic that feels reminiscent of an old picture for which you have an old story, then you will be drawn into playing it out that way just as Betsey was. Perhaps someone else in Betsey's situation could look at Nancy and say, "Look, lady, I'd really like to do this job for you but this is my limit. Please don't push me past here." You can stick up for yourself in a reasonable way. People who can say this find their way with bad bosses and make it work well enough. Then there are other people who become completely stirred up. They feel totally trapped. You can point to the external trap—yes, it's true—but for them as for Betsey much of it comes from the inside.

It could even be that Betsey is invoking these negative feelings—including the hostility from her boss. Sometimes, when people become doormats, that behavior enrages others and begs them to act out. Then those people feel awful about doing that. The natural response is to get rid of the cause of those feelings, and so it wouldn't be unrealistic if Betsey's boss fired Betsey for making her feel like such a witch. You can set up a dynamic that gets the other person to treat you more and more aggressively. This is actually called projective identification—when you behave in a certain way and are in a relationship that draws from the other person the very things you can't bear to feel. In that way, you actually create the very response you most fear. For Betsey, it was "I am your doormat, please wipe your feet on me." But if Betsey sets her limits, her boss may feel she is dealing with an adult and not feel compelled to act so badly toward her.

Practicing the Second Tool

After you have located your biggest conflict, tell another version of it without blaming anyone. Use action verbs—I did this, then I did that. Fantasize about what else you could have done in the situation. Look at those fantasies and see what need you have that those fantasies fulfill. Try to remember other times in your life when you have felt the same way.

Tool 3. Look, Don't Judge

Whenever we have to face some hard truths about ourselves and can't see ourselves as the victims of others, we step in and judge ourselves—usually as harshly as possible. This is precisely what Sydney did. She condemned herself for being an unappreciative cold fish. This kind of thinking only seals in the story. Who wants to examine anything if that search ends in self-disgust? No one. We have to practice empathy for ourselves.

It is impossible to become aware of our stories without empathy. Empathy is different from forgiveness. Empathizing with yourself means standing in your shoes at the tough time. It means going back to your childhood with adult eyes and seeing what it was that made you develop the story you did. Once Sydney saw her need to keep from being abandoned again, she was able to go back to the moment her father left and with an adult perspective see that she was way too young to have been the source of her parents' problems.

When you look at yourself without judging, some of the characteristics you may not like about yourself become much more understandable. Of course it was easier for Sydney to act aloof than to risk being hurt. Being overly self-sufficient and independent allowed Sydney to survive her childhood. The practice of empathy leads to forgiveness, but it also allows you to see the roots of your personality clearly. It's about that moment when you say, "Ah, I get where this came from." Then you can separate the child from the adult and say, "I'm an adult now and I have control over my life. I don't have to keep repeating the same patterns of behavior over and over again."

Without empathy, we can't make the leap from the present behavior to its origins at the beginning of our stories. When we revisit our original conflicts, we must remember that our behavior, our stories, and our personalities resulted from our desire to hold on to those we loved. The negative feelings that were natural consequences of hurtful situations didn't go away when we buried them but emerged as our personalities. We can't possibly begin to untangle these threads without treating ourselves with compassion and kindness.

When we treat ourselves with empathy, it allows us to short-circuit the defensive behavior that rushes in when we feel the truth poking through our stories. If we can look at our behavior without criticizing it, we won't get sidetracked by the need to judge. The goal is to understand. There is a very judgmental part of all of us that develops in childhood at the developmental stage when we are learning right from wrong. We need this ability in order to make distinctions about people's behavior in a civilized world, but we can also turn it in on ourselves and get lost in being harshly critical and thus distract ourselves from true understanding. Examining our stories and our behavior is not an exercise in beating ourselves up. Instead, we want to be able to explore our self-judgments, examine them, and expose how inconsistent they are with reality. I hear perfectly normal-weight women calling themselves "fat," indecisive women calling themselves "weak," emotionally needy women calling themselves "frigid." Judgments exaggerate and therefore obscure the truth. It is impossible to consider and make use of constructive criticism from yourself or others if all criticisms are received as harsh pronouncements of how terrible you are.

If we're committed to seeing what created our behaviors, adding a new and distracting layer of self-recrimination is nothing more than a delaying tactic. It's like starting a brush fire so we don't have to see that the house has burned down.

In Sydney's case, the easiest thing in the world for her to do as a card-carrying Dependent was to push the "play" button on the tape that said, "It's not safe to let anyone see how much I need them. I am not good enough for someone to stick around. If I weren't so damn needy, everything would be okay." But if she could really look at that tape's purpose, she'd see she was just trying to shield herself from the anxious feelings that led to the twisted story she'd created to stay connected to her father, which she could do only by making herself wrong and him right. The unconscious story does not want to be exposed, and it will invent just about any story to keep it from the light of day.

Practicing the Third Tool

When you find yourself in a state of vigorous self-condemnation, stop and examine the specific accusations and see how realistic they are. Are you really so undeserving of love and recognition? Imagine yourself giving those messages to another person. You would probably think that you were being overly harsh and critical. Ask yourself why it's okay for you to think of yourself that way.

As you practice these three tools, you will find that you will have become aware of how and when your old story controls your actions. This is how emotional pain converts into insight and understanding. Once you become aware of your story and personality, you will start to see their fingerprints in every relationship you have—your work, your loved ones, and yourself. When you are conscious that you are trying to fulfill old needs in current circumstances, you start to make different decisions—adult decisions based on who you are and what you need *today*, not who you were or what you needed as a child. You will start getting glimpses of the freedom and authenticity that lie ahead and begin to feel in control of your life—maybe for the first time. This is an exciting moment, but your new consciousness is only half the process—now you are ready to overcome your old story and rewrite a new, real life.

Chapter Seven

FOUR STEPS TO DEFEATING YOUR STORY

No matter how powerful insights may be, simply being aware of our stories does not guarantee change. Seeing how we have been stuck in patterns and old behaviors does not eliminate the old anxieties, hurts, and fears that make us act out very old patterns. Certainly, seeing with adult eyes how we continue to build our lives by protecting ourselves against very old conflicts brings some relief. Understanding how we've become Dependents or Superachievers certainly helps us spot self-destructive behaviors that cause us emotional pain. That awareness allows us the possibility of choosing new actions. But spotting patterns is different from overcoming them. Our core conflicts, the ones that form our personalities, lie stubbornly embedded within us. Awareness of them may cause them to shrink, but we won't overcome them unless we take new actions based on who we really are today.

When we act differently, we lessen our stories' powers. We can override the automatic-pilot feature that directs us to act in preprogrammed ways and begin expanding the repertoire of possibilities. We can then rewrite our stories from our new adult perspective. We can make the decision to use our insights to rewrite their messages. No permanent change happens without this. The good news is that not only is rewriting possible, but it also brings tremendous relief. Each time we stop before we repeat our unconscious patterns, we immediately step into a much larger world filled with new choices and expanded possibilities. This new world is full of excitement, power, and freedom.

Here's the dirty little secret—as children, our stories told us we could hold on to love and feel emotional order and safety if we acted in a certain way. But, as adults, the opposite happens. The stories rob us of ever being able to feel loved. Because we have built our personalities conditionally—"If I act in such-and-such a way, then I will be loved and not abandoned"—deep inside we know that people then only love us because of our actions, not because of who we really are. It may never get consciously articulated, but we really do fear that we have presented people with our false fronts, the ones we think people will love. When someone loves that personality, we fear that if that person knew who we *really* were, they would leave us, reject us, betray us, condemn us—in short, we would be exposed for the inadequate or unlovable children we were when our primary emotional needs weren't fulfilled.

What a devastating reality stories create—they deny us the possibility of ever feeling loved for who we really are. Rewriting our stories, letting our real selves take center stage, is a huge risk when we have lived our lives running from taking the chance of exposure. But it is ultimately the only way any of us can experience true intimacy, feel truly seen for who we are and loved and understood.

Mourning the Loss of the Fictional You

Making the decision to move beyond the limits of our stories means risking just about everything—our identities, our personalities, our rules for the way we operate out in the world. Interrupting their instructions means opening ourselves up and exposing the inner workings. It means becoming anxious and vulnerable. It means abandoning the protective armor we donned as children. It means being willing to examine the people we became as a result of our stories and to give up the parts that are holding us back.

As we contemplate what it takes to clear away the parts of our personalities that block our authentic strengths and abilities, we might feel profound sadness, slide into brief depression, and have moments of sharp anxiety. Making a decision to change means giving up the security we have clung to for many years. That's why we have to be pretty miserable to contemplate such a tall task. But as we slip and backslide—as we all do—remember to keep your mind prioritized. Your story will fight to hold on, but slowly and surely, the treasures it is hiding will be revealed.

If you feel worse for a while after beginning this process, know that you're in the right place. It's to be expected. Remember underneath every story lie profound fears:

- I am broken and will be abandoned.
- I am inadequate and unlovable.
- Life is not fair, so I will be denied the love I seek.

These fears are enough to scare us back into that pretzel shape we contorted ourselves into to hold on to the sources of love all those years ago. But remember how constricting it is to live like that. Remember the promise of being loved for your authentic self. The unconscious will try with all its might to stay hidden and in control. That's why it's so important to remember to treat yourself with kindness, with empathy.

When we become willing to risk the personalities we built so we wouldn't have to live with these fears, we are rewarded with the unshakable and profound understanding that we, as adults, are lovable, adequate, and as able as the next person to get what we need and want out of our lives.

Four Steps to Overcoming Your Story

Living your new story takes a lifetime. But coming up with the new story line, one that accurately reflects your authentic self, can be done in four steps:

1. Tell yourself your old story.
2. See the story's cost.
3. Rewrite your story.
4. Take new actions.

Step 1. Tell Yourself Your Old Story

Let's go back for a moment and remind ourselves about the primary needs and the stories and personalities that come out of them: attachment, individuation, expression, and attunement. Remember that when there is a conflict or a lack of fulfillment at each emotionally needy stage—*for whatever reason*—it creates the story whose entire purpose is to keep us connected to that loving source. When you tell yourself your old story, ask yourself which one of these needs (it could be more than one!) sits at the center. It will help you see what you were willing to do to get these needs met. It will also help you evaluate what in your present life really is meeting these needs that you couldn't see until now because your story was in the way.

1. *Attachment:* This is the very earliest need for love and security. Any frustration of this need and your story will tell you, "I can't depend on anyone but myself. I'm too needy"—the theme song of the Dependent.

2. *Individuation:* When your attempts to become autonomous and to create healthy boundaries are met with anger or disapproval, you end up with the Self-defeater's theme songs: "I can't do anything wrong, or I'll pay. I can't take it when someone gets mad at me. If I let them win, they'll like me."

3. *Expression:* Superachievers never felt accepted for who they were— so performance becomes all-important for them. Their theme songs from humanity's greatest hits sound like this: "If I'm not number one, then why bother? People don't give me the credit I deserve."

4. *Attunement:* When we aren't seen and understood for who we are, we literally feel out of tune and try to become the people we perceive will bring us back into harmony with other's visions of us. Perfectionists tried to stay attuned by following "the rules" that were laid down for them. They internalized these rules so that their stories tell them, "There is a right way and a wrong way to do

everything. I must do the right thing because doing wrong will lead to calamity." Also, Competitors come out of this need's frustrations with their themes of "If only I were thinner, richer, more successful, or prettier, I would be happy." Or "When I'm married (or married to the right person), I'll be happy."

These are tremendous reductions of our personalities—we are really much more elaborate than this. But I offer these shorthands simply to help you as you tell yourself your old story.

Della tidied her desk and was about to leave work to make our 5:30 P.M. appointment. She was exhausted; it had been a trying few days. She spent the early part of the week rushing to complete a proposal letter for her boss who was anxious to have it done *yesterday*. She delivered it in record time, but it sat on his desk for three days. Now, at this late hour, he handed the letter back to her with tons of edits that had to be made right away. "This is a sloppy job," her boss told her angrily. "I expected more. After you get this done, we're going to have to review your work." Caught between the need to please and the need to take care of herself, Della erupted, "That's it. I quit! I can't take this anymore." And she marched out the door.

By the time she got to my office, she was absolutely panicking and crying: What had she done? She needed this job. There was no other job like it. She'd never work again! Oh, would her boss take her back if she begged him and apologized profusely?

Della and I had been working together for a while. She understood that she was a Self-defeater with a strong streak of Dependent. She'd had a very critical father who always felt she didn't apply herself in her schoolwork. Her father's constant criticism extended to her mother, who responded to her husband by becoming distant and depressed. As she grew older, Della responded to the criticism by proving her father right: She would do a good job at something for a while, but the minute that more work or longer hours was involved, she would do something to sabotage all the work she had done to that point. Her fight with her boss was a perfect example. Instead of just doing the work, she had now potentially lost her job or, at a minimum, her boss's respect.

I pointed out that she'd had an out-of-proportion reaction to the situation—as irritating and disrespectful as it might have been—and that was a clear sign she was being controlled by an old story. Her outburst was not just at her boss but at someone else. But who? I asked her to tell me her old story. She began by using the three tools we talked about in the last chapter. I asked her to:

1. *Sit, don't act.* To become aware, she needed to quietly locate the current conflict and feel the feelings. This part was a no-brainer. She'd just had the huge fight and was full of two emotions—fury and fear. Fury at being asked to do more and fear that she would lose her connection to her work and its security.

2. *Shift from victim to storyteller.* Next, she revisited the conflict without blaming. She said she felt her work was either so unimportant that it (and she) had been ignored for three days, or she feared her work (and she) had been so inadequate that she wanted to get away from the feelings that resulted as quickly as she possibly could. Her eruption accomplished that. Adding to everything else was a sense of impotent rage. She was so angry but felt she couldn't express it appropriately without the fear of getting fired!

3. *Look, don't judge.* I asked Della to find a time in her childhood

when she had had these same feelings. She had to do this without blaming herself for any behavior that might have resulted as a consequence. She immediately went back to a time in the third grade when her standardized test scores were too low for her to qualify for the gifted and talented program. Her father had been so cruel about it, referring to her as "my idiot child" and wondering out loud to her mother if it were possible that Della was "the milkman's daughter." Della became extremely fearful when she heard this, thinking that she was going to be rejected and abandoned by her father. She tried to explain that it was only one test and she'd had an ear infection while taking it, but her father came down on her like a ton of bricks. She shut up, realizing it was better to take the criticism than the anger. She looked to her mother for support, but her mother responded by removing herself emotionally, which Della experienced as an abandonment.

These tools allowed Della to connect her current conflict to her old story. She could see that the part of her story that was Dependent instructed her to please an authority figure so she wouldn't be separated: "I have to fulfill all your needs, or I'll be abandoned. The other part of the story involved an inability to tolerate anger: "I can't do anything wrong or I'll pay, and I can't take your being mad at me." She cut off her nose to spite her boss's face in a classic Self-defeater move.

Step 2. See The Story's Cost

When we defend ourselves, we keep others out. Each person pays the price of living with a false or compensatory self. This distortion keeps us from fully experiencing our authenticity, our gifts, our talents; it keeps us from real trust, ease, and intimacy with others. What price do you think you have paid? Try to imagine what your life would be like without your story's imposed boundaries.

Della's price was pretty clear: In order to stay connected to the one she loved who also provided her with security, she had to never show anger and to never succeed. The first one is easy to understand from her relationship with her critical father. But the second one is a little sneakier. Remember, she'd been ignored for three days in her mind. By having a fight with her boss, by overreacting, she created a strong emotional connection to him. One that hurt her in the end, but the unconscious doesn't care. It's a connection-seeking missile, and it will aim repeatedly at anything that its sensors report might feel like the original source of intimacy. We all know people who get along by fighting with each other. To them, that's a form of maintaining intimacy—not a healthy one, but a bond nonetheless.

Della's story has cost her this job, as well as other jobs and past relationships. It has kept her from achieving at work, and it has kept her from growing maturely as a human being who is capable of learning and improving. Each time she feels she's been criticized (and she's very sensitive to anything that even smacks of disapproval), she cuts off the relationship or employment and moves on, starting the process all over again. As a consequence, she's thirty-two with no man and no job on the horizon.

Seeing her story's cost, Della is finally miserable enough to prioritize her mind and take the risk of changing her story.

Step 3. Rewrite Your Story

Take the message from your story—any one of humanity's greatest hits—like "I can't depend on anyone but myself" or "If only I were prettier, I'd be happy"—and turn it inside out. What would your story be like if you were not only adequate but also lovable?

For Della, turning her messages inside out means this: Instead of feeling "I can't take it when somebody is mad at me" and "I can't do anything wrong or I'll pay," both of which are built around her fear of not being adequate, which results in abandonment and rejection, Della tells herself, "Just because he's angry at me doesn't mean I'm going to be left alone" and "I made a mistake but *I* am not the mistake." When she does this, she immediately feels the panic in her subside. She sees why she overreacted. Her old story told her that she's a stupid person who's going to be abandoned. But that's not what's really happening. According to the new message, she sees that her boss has a temper, and perhaps she has to work a bit more carefully. By rewriting her story, the adult picks up the pen and takes charge of the narrative. By definition, this adult is much more able, independent, and powerful than the child author of the old story. Very different consequences result.

Let me show you what I mean by rewriting humanity's greatest hits:

- "I can't depend on anyone but myself" becomes "I can ask for what I need."
- "If only I were thinner, richer, more successful, or prettier, I would be happy" becomes "I like myself just the way I am."
- "There's a right way and a wrong way to do everything, and his way is wrong" becomes "There's no right or wrong. It's safe to choose what works best for me or to compromise."

- "I can't do anything wrong, or I'll pay" becomes "Everyone makes mistakes, and I will be loved even if I do make them."

- "When I'm married (or married to the right person), I'll be happy" becomes "I don't need a man in order to be happy."

- "I'm too needy" becomes "It's all right to have needs, and not all needs can be fulfilled by one person."

- "If I'm not number one, then why bother?" becomes "I am adequate just as I am."

- "I can't take it when someone gets mad at me" becomes "Everyone gets angry. I can withstand anger and be okay."

- "My problems are all my parents' (or husband's or boss's) fault" becomes "I am an adult, responsible for my own actions and reactions."

- "People don't give me the credit I deserve" becomes "I know when I've done a good job, and I don't need someone to tell me."

- "If I let them win, they'll like me" becomes "I don't have to be a doormat to be loved."

We all have our own versions of these themes, and I offer these just as a guide to get you started. Now, think about your old story and the messages you are aware of. Then ask yourself a few questions:

- *What is my old story telling me to do in this situation?* Is it telling you to stay silent when you're angry? Change your clothes to feel loved? Excel to be recognized?

- *What is the cost I pay if I do this?* Do I eat compulsively when afraid? Do I feel men only love me for my body? Do I have no friends because I always have to win?

- *What other options can I imagine?* What if I told him his comments made me mad? What if I didn't put makeup on first thing in the morning? What if I wasn't always right?

- *How would that change what will happen?* Will I have a meaningful interchange, making him aware of his criticism so he won't do it again? Will I feel that he's interested in *me* and not just my breasts? Will I be able to be a peer and an equal and have more friends?

- *What will I gain by doing this?* I will see that it's okay to be appropriately annoyed or angry and that people won't leave me if I do. I will see that I'm lovable just as I am without the sexy clothes or makeup. I will see that I am adequate just as I am, and I don't have to be number one to be loved and accepted.

Once you answer that last question, you have overcome your old story. You can rewrite your new story from the starting point of the mature individual you are today. You will ground your actions not on what you fear is inadequacy or unlovableness—all the faulty conclusions underlying your old story—but on the real person you are today.

Step 4. Take New Actions

When we overcome our old stories, we can break free of old behaviors. But we have to act differently in order to make the new story real. These new actions will feel awkward, risky, or even unsafe. They come from the new story line and will feel counterintuitive. Don't let discomfort stop you, but don't do anything dangerous or brash; remember—sit, don't act. Use your common sense and think each new action through. Perhaps you can find a trusted friend with whom to discuss your new behavior.

I asked Della what new actions she could take based on her new story. She felt that the first thing she would do is see if she could undo some of the damage her outburst caused without groveling. She would apologize and do the best job she could with the edited proposal. Going forward, she would pause before any reaction, knowing that her response to any anger or criticism would automatically come from the default settings of the old story. She would learn to see what the criticisms were before jumping to the conclusion she was no good—something that enraged her.

If you don't make the decision to act differently, you will immediately revert to the old story's behavior. Like staying on a diet, each time you say no to food that makes you fat and yes to food that makes you fit, you are reinforcing yourself. It is harder in the beginning but it gets easier as you go along—*if* you stay with it.

The reason you have to act, not just think at this point, is that you have to show yourself that you have more options than you believe about yourself. Once you do something differently and the world doesn't end—which it never does—you begin to see the price you've been paying for letting your story control you. Once you take an action that counters the story instead of supporting it, you realize how much freedom you gain, how many more choices you have, and how much creativity exists. The energy that you have spent to keep everything in check can now be used to express yourself authentically as an adult. You will also have an immediate respite from all the tension and anger that built up because who you are as an adult has taken a backseat to your childhood fears for too long. When you aren't sitting on a mountain of rage and anxiety, you can be more giving—to your spouse, to your kids, and to yourself.

The good news here is that, no matter what your personality type is, these four steps will help you overcome your old behaviors—the ones that are causing your distress. The next five chapters go through the process of rewriting each type's story. I urge you not to read only the one you think applies to you. I have seen more patients than I can count, and I promise you I have never seen anyone with just one story—we all have a potent mix of each. And remember to read with kindness! These stories have gotten you where you are today, and we owe them a debt of gratitude. You do yourself no good if you beat yourself up because of old behaviors. Hey, that's a story in itself!

Chapter Eight

DEFEATING THE DEPENDENT STORY

Sydney is at the crisis point. Two nights ago at dinner, Brian announced that he wanted to put the wedding plans on hold. The fiasco over the surprise weekend really gave him second thoughts. He loves Sydney but doesn't think he can handle being married to someone who is so independent and giving one day and then snappish and aloof the next. He thought his love would calm her down, but it seems to him that it's only made things worse.

Sitting in my office, Sydney is clearly ready to do something—anything—to hold on to Brian. She really does love him. It's just that she's so damn scared. Sydney knows intellectually what her story is—she recognizes that her Dependent personality, which has given her security for many years now, threatens her very happiness. She has made a decision to risk that story to save her relationship.

Rewriting Sydney's Dependent story means expanding the way she sees and values herself. It's all out of whack. Her Dependent personality and self-worth are built on these themes: "I am entirely giving. I am needed. I am somebody who gives all to those who need me. I am sweet and compliant." Indeed, the Dependent *is* all these things. If you identify with this, don't worry; these things you like about yourself won't go away in your new story. But they will get balanced out so that your life becomes livable and you won't feel like everyone around you is sucking you dry.

When you change your message from "I don't need anything. I have to do everything alone, because I will be abandoned if I reveal my neediness" to "Everyone has needs, and I won't be abandoned if I tell you mine. I can have limits if you show me yours," suddenly the door opens wide and lets in all the love and attention you crave but were afraid to ask for. You can begin to form true intimate bonds because they won't feel like they have the potential to obliterate you. But it isn't going to happen in the all-or-nothing way you expect.

The truth is that whether or not a Dependent acknowledges it, you have needs. It's just that you couldn't express them without feeling they were so overwhelming to others that they would leave you. Now, as an adult, you get a chance to try saying, "I am someone who can express my hurt or disappointment. I can express my needs and ask for them to be fulfilled." That rewrites your self-image as: *"I am somebody who has needs. I am somebody who has and can express aggression and anger. I can ask for my needs (which are not a bottomless well) to be fulfilled."*

For a Dependent, those sentences are positively subversive. It can feel like it will surely produce the very thing you most fear. But if you've begun to see how you've built your life around not appearing needy or angry, then you are ready to rewrite your story.

Step 1. Tell Yourself Your Old Story

I ask Sydney to try to identify herself as a person who has a history of either being abandoned or having unmet needs. It's important that she recognize her history so that she can empathize with her story's origins. I don't want her to wallow in the past but to simply try and observe what it was that went on at an early age that gave her the message that wanting or acting out in any way made her an unbearable burden on her parents. She quickly recalled how she never directly asked for anything from her father for fear he would treat her like he treated her mother and ultimately leave them both. Sadly enough, in spite of her twisted efforts, that is precisely what happened, and when it did, her conviction that she pushed him away with her neediness cemented her story. Sydney remembers that her mother's response was to depend on Sydney completely for emotional support in the wake of her father's departure. Thus, Sydney's story had two models of neediness—in the first, it caused abandonment, and in the second, it meant she would be swamped by the needs of others.

Now you try. Look back and see what incidents in your past have led you to the conclusion that it's better to do things yourself than to depend on others and to be wary of others' needs because they can suck you dry. See if you can find the roots of the behavior that has you doing everything for everyone. Do you go and go and go and then collapse? Does your health give out dramatically? Underneath all those behaviors lies your old story. If your personality has a heavy streak of Dependent in it, you will find the sources pretty quickly.

If you feel safe doing this, try to experience the sadness and the pain that accompany your fears of not being lovable enough or too needy.

Do you feel chronically frustrated when your needs are overlooked or you're ignored or don't have what others have? Do you imagine if you allow yourself to be aware of your needs, it will open a Pandora's box of neediness? Do you think you have a bottomless well of needs that will cause anyone who sees that to run away? Try to see how those feelings—or indeed, just the *fear* of those feelings—trigger your tried-and-true behavior patterns. If you can't hold on to friends or boy-friends, and are a bit of a loner at heart, try to sit in the feelings that propel you into being "the one who has to do it all" or "everybody's rock" or "always the bridesmaid and never the bride." Try to think about all the times you were angry because you didn't feel people saw what a wonderful person you were or when you didn't feel safe speak-ing up for yourself, asserting yourself, or getting angry when anger was called for. In all likelihood, you are sitting on a mountain of anger because you always have to "do everything" for yourself and others, while at the same time you live in terror of others knowing you feel that way. Try to experience that anger and that fear and then imagine a greater strength as you try on the idea that you can be more assertive about what you want and feel.

Step 2. See the Story's Cost

To be free of the old story, Dependents need to see what cost they are paying for the constant giving and hyper-independent living. When we look at the story's costs, we also have to see its benefits. The story worked for a long time—that's why it's hard to give up. Let's look at Sydney. Her personality has been a great asset to her. In the beginning, it helped her literally survive her father's departure and her mother's dependency. As she got older, she was highly motivated to do well in school and get a good job because she knew she couldn't depend on anyone else to take care of her—it was always going to be up to her. She makes friends who are happy to have someone so dependable in their lives. Maybe they feel it's a bit of a one-way street, but Sydney's personality has attracted people who are comfortable "taking" from others. So far, so good.

But now, as Sydney matures, what happens when she starts wanting intimate connections in friendship and in love? What happens when she gets to a point in her career when she has to be part of a team or manage people? She doesn't have the ability to give and take. She can't let people close to her for all the reasons we've discussed (which is why she's still single), and because she has no ability to create a healthy boundary, she isn't well equipped to take on anyone's emotional needs (like children!). At her job, what was independence has slipped into standoffishness and micromanagement, which aren't doing much for her performance at work. Finally, her health has given out because she's collapsing in on herself, and it is the only way she can allow any caretaking. Sydney's story has cost her dearly.

What has your story cost you? Can you see how your themes, your personality, have both the positive and the negative? Can you see how traits that served you well came directly out of your story but have begun to turn on you later in life? Taking an empathetic look at your story will let you see what you've paid emotionally in loneliness, exhaustion, depression, or just plain chronic malaise.

Step 3. Rewrite Your Story

Keeping in mind that your old story told you to express no needs, try turning that story inside out. Change it to *"I am somebody who has needs. I am somebody who has and can express my feelings. I am someone who is entitled to have her needs fulfilled as well as fulfilling the needs of others."*

What impact would this have on Sydney's actions? In a word: huge. Let's go back to Brian's country-inn weekend surprise. Sydney had been struggling with problems at work that week. Her boss had told her that one of her staff complained that Sydney wouldn't let him just do his job. That's one of the reasons Brian had conceived the idea of going away. If Sydney could feel she was entitled to a little caretaking, what would have happened? She probably would have flung her arms around his neck, kissed him everywhere she could, and gotten into the car thinking she was the luckiest woman on earth to be marrying such a thoughtful, caring fellow.

Notice that nothing Brian did is different in this scenario. But a change in perspective—a rewriting of a central message—allows intimacy, pleasure, and plain old happiness. All of those emotions are blocked by the old story and personality.

As you rewrite your story, an army of reasons you shouldn't trust the new message will arise (they're all listed in Chapter Thirteen). Their purpose is to get you to hold on to the old story by telling you there really isn't a problem or that you're being selfish, you're risking too much, that the other person is a jerk—on and on. This is completely natural and to be expected—the old story isn't going to just roll over and give up without a fight. So hang in there and recognize the resistance, but put the new message into your life anyway.

Step 4. Take New Actions

When you start to act, ask yourself if you are acting according to your real story, your balanced story. If you are doing something to keep someone near you but it involves denying yourself—try again. I asked Sydney what new actions she could take based on her new story. Here's a short list of what she came up with:

- I will let Brian give me breakfast in bed.
- I will let him pleasure me.
- I will not micromanage my staff but will delegate appropriate work to them.
- I will set limits with my mother and all her requests.
- Once a day, I will ask for something I really need—whether it's help with a project, having lunch with a friend, or a hug from Brian.

Not a bad start. Now, you try. There are a few things you can do to get started. If you aren't ready to ask others for what you need, begin by giving yourself what you wish the world would give you. It's important to find methods of soothing and nurturing yourself and fulfilling your own needs. This can be something as simple as going out to dinner when you don't want to cook, reading a book, going to the doctor, or getting your hair cut. Being able to do things for yourself is very important. It's not indulgent or selfish. What it does is train you to recognize a need and know it can be met without the world order crashing down around your ears.

Practice asking for help. Taking new actions means learning to reach out and ask for help directly in your social and family relationships. You must learn to be able to say to a loved one, "I do need things. Could you help me?" It won't take long for you to see that far from causing abandonment, this will strengthen your adult relationships. By reaching out and making more active attempts to not hide what you think people can't handle, you will have more intimate relationships. Other people will find it gratifying to be able to satisfy your needs, too.

Another new action involves learning to be alone. Dependents need to work on increasing their tolerance for this. Because of the fear of being abandoned, Dependents are excellent at being with people all the time, busily fulfilling others' needs and feeling resentful about the fact that they don't feel there's any reciprocity or intimacy. Dependents need to be able to enjoy solitude not as a reaction to people's real or imagined callousness to them but so they can see that being alone is not the same as being abandoned. Tremendous strength and clarity come from seeing that spending time by yourself is not the same as being abandoned.

What's the payoff for all this work? A simple and powerful one. I promise that if you practice these four steps, that if you commit to putting them into your life, you will be able to have the very intimacy and connection you felt you were denied as a child.

Don't be surprised if you backslide into old, repetitive patterns. Overcoming your old story is a process, and it takes time. But gradually, each time you act on your new story, you strengthen your chances at having the love and attachment you need and deserve.

Chapter Nine

DEFEATING THE
SUPERACHIEVER STORY

Andrew sits in my office with a war-weary expression. He feels he is being attacked from all sides—his wife, Junie, is accusing him of making their son neurotic. His mother feels Andrew's problems began the day he married Junie. The chief of surgery has asked to see him again next week for what, Andrew is sure, is another nuisance complaint from his lazy nursing staff.

But it's his son's problems that have pierced his protective story. Adam clearly is having adjustment problems in school. Besides being made fun of for his facial tic, the kids call Adam a know-it-all and aren't playing with him or inviting him to play dates. Enough of Junie's accusations of "like father like son" have crept into Andrew's consciousness that he's now willing to look at his story.

Sadly, the Superachiever story can often make them unsympathetic to others because their personalities appear grandiose and self-confident.

"I know more, I am smarter, I am the most capable," the story goes. On a surface level, many, like Andrew, will have lives that warrant all those feelings. Rewriting their stories begins when they can acknowledge that underneath all that surety and accomplishment, they've built their lives over a yawning canyon of feelings of worthlessness, depression, and aloneness. Certainly this is what Andrew sees when he looks at his son. And it strikes a familiar chord inside him. Indeed, this story and many of the real achievements that come from it are designed to prove to Superachievers and the world that they are worth something—quite a bit in fact. But because they are building their lives in reaction to feelings of insufficiency, a vulnerable hollowness lies at the center of their stories. Inside, Superachievers know that they criticize themselves a lot and don't trust others. When they can see and admit that they use their achievements, successes, or activities that garner success to try to fend off all those negative feelings about themselves, their new stories can begin.

Rewriting the Superachiever's story means giving them the message and the means to feel they are sufficient—lovable—and whole without all the accomplishments, accolades, and awards.

Step 1. Tell Yourself Your Old Story

Everything in Andrew's story is designed to fend off his feelings of insignificance. The fantasies of grandness, the sense of entitlement, the superiority, all cover up his fears that inside he deserves absolutely nothing. In fact, all this being superspecial, godlike, and grand is really just a false personality—a destructive ego that's out of control. Yet he needs to be able to see that who he really is and the personality his story created are different. But if your biggest fear is that you are nothing inside nothing, it's pretty hard to acknowledge the false persona and begin to peel away the story's messages. What lies beneath is too frightening to contemplate. If you are a Superachiever, it's important to treat yourself with the utmost in empathy. In the past, your need to feel you were being paid attention to was frustrated. All children need to feel loved for who they are, and—for whatever reason—you did not experience that with the adults in your life.

To get to Andrew's old story, I first ask him to locate his most immediate conflict. He pauses; there are so many and he feels so embattled. But the one where his energies run highest seems to be his ongoing tug-of-war with Junie. She doesn't acknowledge what a fine father he is, what a strong provider, what a superior life he's giving his wife and kid. All she seems to see are his downsides.

Without looking for an action to take, I ask Andrew to feel the feeling that comes out of this conflict: His face immediately flushes. Andrew is furious that he is being so unappreciated. But when I ask him to shift his perspective from victim in the conflict to storyteller, he has a hard time of it. Finally, he comes up with a version of the story that says that he needs Junie's approval to feel good about himself. Her withholding of it—for whatever complicated reasons, some of which are her own story—has caused Andrew to rely even more heavily on his achievements to bolster himself up. Inside, he struggles with feeling like a zero.

I ask Andrew to try to reach back into the past and see where the phrase "If I'm not number one, then I'm nothing at all" applied. Very quickly, he recalls a moment in grade school, third grade to be precise, where his report card mentioned that his writing skills—both form and content—were not at grade level. "My mother hit the roof. She wanted me to be successful and told me I never would be if I couldn't write. I showed her. I became a doctor! They're successful *and* they have bad handwriting!" The incident may have been small, and doubtless his story started long before he was even conscious of it, but seeing that moment with empathetic eyes allowed him to see his story. That to gain his mother's love and affection, he became what she wanted. And the more he became a success, the more love he seemed to get—until it began to backfire in his marriage with Junie.

Step 2. See the Story's Cost

When you're a child and you keep getting the message that who you are is wrong, it creates tremendous feelings of hurt and injury. Not surprisingly, as adults, Superachievers carry with them tremendous fears of being criticized or rejected again. Their days are filled with suspicion and distrust of others that the same thing will happen. They keep proving their abilities in order to fend off their anxiety that someone will see through their facades and think they are as worthless as they actually feel they are deep inside. They use up tremendous energy trying to prove to themselves and others that they are worth loving.

This is certainly the case with Andrew. He works constantly—if he's not on call at the hospital, he goes anyway. But now he's even being criticized for that. He can't win, and the conflict inside him is causing him to act out in rage at his coworkers and to feel increasingly depressed at home. He looks at his staff and sees incompetence. He looks at his wife and sees a nagging, affected, spoiled woman. All these extensions of himself also never measure up. Not surprisingly, Andrew rarely feels satisfied with life and has redoubled his efforts to get to someplace where everything and everyone will be good enough—a place where he can then feel adequate. But because of his story, that place does not exist. He is living in a constant state of frustration, self-criticism, and disappointment.

So what's the cost to Andrew? Where to begin? If you are a Super-achiever like Andrew, you pay dearly for your story in lost intimacy, in emotional security, in any sense of real satisfaction. Because you need to feel superior to feel safe, by definition you can't have true unguarded closeness with another person or experience vulnerability and care. Relationships are power struggles—you have to know most or know best. Thus, in relationships, you often choose people who don't have the education, experience, information, or skills that you do, or you often remind your partners that you, the Superachiever, knows more/better/best. It's hard to have an intimate and equal relationship on those terms.

The Superachiever story also robs you of any real emotional security. If everything you do depends on *what* you do and how well you do it, that's a pretty conditional life. It precludes your ever feeling adequate or enough when you aren't performing or excelling or extolling your own virtues. So even when you succeed, you can't take real pleasure in your success because each one is just another notch in an endless belt that measures self-worth.

Finally, your story denies you any real sense of satisfaction—with yourself or anyone else. You will never be good enough; you will never be appreciated enough. Your spouse or job or kids will never be good enough or grand enough because you are looking to them for something that you can't give yourself. The message and understanding that no matter what you do or don't do, you are lovable and acceptable the way you are only come when you rewrite your story.

Step 3. Rewrite Your Story

Rewriting the Superachiever story means turning your most cherished beliefs inside out. It means accepting that you, everybody, and everything have limits. In accepting those limits, you can create a more realistic view both of yourself and of other people. You can also have a more realistic acceptance of what you're really capable of and what reasonable ambitions might be. In the new story, as a Superachiever you can take a realistic look at what you are and aren't capable of and create reasonable expectations for your achievements and relationships. The new story lets you look at your own weaknesses without immediately becoming a nothing or a nobody. Because the Superachiever story tells you that you have to be the best or you don't exist, rewriting that central piece allows you the extremely valuable ability to look at yourself honestly and know yourself.

I ask Andrew if he can replace his story of having to achieve (and be recognized for) "greatness" with this story instead: *"I have faults and others have faults, but that doesn't mean we're not worthy of love."* This new story allows him to express understanding and respect of other people that he hadn't expressed in the past. Being able to accept faults in himself will give him a regard, a respect, and an empathic understanding of himself. This is something he will need to work toward accepting. Andrew needs to be able to accept care and affection from other people and not criticize their form. If his new story appreciates that we aren't perfect and we all have limits, he will allow so much more love into his life because limits and imperfections won't threaten his very being anymore.

Your goal as a Superachiever is to rewrite your story so you can say, *"Yes, I'm not perfect. But I'm not so horrendous, either. I'm somewhere in the middle just like everyone else. I can love someone who is not perfect. If they're not perfect, it doesn't mean they're terrible or that I am by extension. I can sympathize with myself that I felt misunderstood and not accepted for who I was and am."* If you can articulate this, you can come to see that, while your past may have been sad and difficult, your armor of perfection has kept out more than just criticism and rejection; it's kept out love. To twist an old phrase, it's better to have loved and been imperfect than never to have been loved at all.

Step 4. Take New Actions

Perhaps the hardest thing for a Superachiever to do is to make a mistake and then admit it. But what liberation comes for you when you can do so. You will quickly see that compassion for your humanity and fallibility not only lessens your anxiety level but also lets other people in closer to you. Another action for the Superachiever is to learn to listen and not sit in judgment. Because of the need to be superior to feel safe, it's only natural that you feel compelled to point out the failings in other people. So, to twist a common phrase, the Superachiever should "Just *not* do it!"

I ask Andrew to put his new story of being able to be imperfect, limited, and sufficient just as he is into his consciousness, and I ask him what new actions he could think of. These are just a few of them:

- I will not look at everything Junie says as coming from ignorance.
- I will listen to the criticism of my coworkers with an open mind without telling them how much more I know.
- I will lay off Adam and let him go at his own pace.
- I will go to counseling with Junie and examine both the problems and the good things I bring to the relationship.
- Once a day, I will acknowledge a mistake and forgive myself for it.

Quite a bit rides on these new actions. If Andrew can put them into place, his relationships will explode in richness and communication. He will immediately reap the rewards of feeling appreciated for who he is, not for his superiority. He will have the emotional security and satisfaction denied to him as long as he is so superior and perfect. Finally, he may be able to stop his son from becoming a Superachiever like he is—or, if he hasn't, then he'll be able to understand and help Adam. Remember that Superachievers often pass along their ways to the next generation. This really frightened Andrew, as he saw his son fall prey to the prison of perfection and self-criticism that plagued his life. Andrew's son's facial tics expressed the deep anxiety Andrew knew all too well. He clearly saw Adam's disease for what it was—the creation of a lifelong story. In order to be real, Andrew needed to accept that he was contributing to his son's nervous condition. By accepting responsibility for a fallible part of himself, he could save his son.

But what about Andrew's marriage? What does his new, real story tell him to do that could save his relationship? When he met Junie, she represented a kind of perfection to him. She was perfectly bohemian and exciting, and as an up-and-coming artist, she had the requisite achievements that Andrew needed in a partner. Over time, though, as she became what he viewed as mundane and mediocre, he lost his interest—rather like that saying, "I don't want to belong to any club that would have me as a member." To reengage in their relationship, Andrew has to see how his old story set him up to be disappointed. By projecting his need to be exceptional on Junie, she couldn't help but let him down later. If he can see Junie for who she is and let her see him with all his foibles, then their marriage will have a chance.

If Andrew rewrites his story to include the fact that we all make mistakes, he will become willing to look and see if maybe he has made a mistake in what he has presented as best for his son. And if he has, to see that error isn't necessarily irrevocable, and Andrew isn't a terrible, horrible person.

As you start to overcome your story, the heaviness that accompanies being trapped in the story will lift. You will get the gift of tremendous energy and enthusiasm. All the time and effort that went into tap dancing for love and appreciation can be channeled into your relationships, your work, and yourself. You will experience peace of mind in quiet moments because you won't have to *do* all the time. As the expression goes, you will be a human *being,* complete and lovable as you are—not a human *doing,* always singing for your supper.

Chapter Ten

DEFEATING THE SELF-DEFEATER STORY

Overcoming the Self-defeater story means coming out of hiding because the essence of that story lies in its indirection. If you are a Self-defeater, you take your anger, aggression, and disappointments out on yourself while wishing you could take them out on others. As I said earlier, you'd gladly cut off your own nose to spite somebody else's face. To rewrite your story, you first have to understand what happened in your life that left you feeling so powerless that this was your only recourse. When you can accept that sabotaging yourself is your expression of hostility and your retaliation for real or imagined hurts, then you are ready to rewrite your story. Deep inside, your story tells you that you aren't good enough, sufficient enough, or lovable enough to be entitled to pleasure or good things. When you overcome your story by rewriting it, you will step out of your self-imposed punishment and enjoy all the good things in life you've felt you didn't deserve.

Now, let's look at Junie, Superachiever Andrew's wife. I ask her to be aware of her old story. Clearly, the biggest conflict in her life is in her marriage, so I want her to find her story there. I ask Junie why she stays in a marriage that is so unfulfilling to her. They hadn't had sex in more than a year, and before that, their sex life hadn't been great. Andrew was emotionally unavailable in addition to being highly critical. An old battle with anorexia had recently begun to resurface as she tried to make herself smaller and smaller, as a way to punish herself and literally disappear from the situation.

Step 1. Tell Yourself Your Old Story

"Why do you think you have to stay in your marriage?" I ask her. My point is not to urge her to leave Andrew. Such a decision is entirely up to her. What I want her to do is see what it is in her story that compels her to cling to something that makes her miserable. "You often describe the feeling you are being punished. Yet, you feel you cannot stop, set limits, or leave. What makes the idea of either changing the relationship or leaving it feel so scary?" I ask, again seeking to draw her attention to her desire for punishment rather than accusing Andrew of dispensing it. I want her to see that she has a choice about feeling trapped—that it is up to her whether she wants to stay or go. Her story restricts her vision and her sense of what's possible. Her response to my questions will help her see that.

"Because I cannot bear to be alone," she says, echoing the response I hear most often when I ask these questions. "Because I can't earn a living or take care of Adam by myself. Because if we split, I'm afraid I'll fall apart. I'm probably getting what I deserve anyway. I can be such a bitch."

There it was—her Self-defeater story's message—"I'm not enough on my own. I still need to be taken care of. I'm really a bad person deserving of punishment." Losing her husband—even if she were the one to leave—would be the proof she knew existed that she wasn't good enough.

If you're a Self-defeater like Junie, you are probably filled with anger that you don't feel safe expressing outwardly. Thus, you either take that anger out on yourself through self-destructive patterns in your health, finances, relationships, or your work life. Or you express anger in a very passive way—by not sticking up for yourself and letting others abuse you (which makes them hate both themselves for doing so and you for egging them into it!). If relationships are a constant reminder that you aren't enough, it's going to make you angry. But if you're a Self-defeater, you got that story directly out of your experience of having tried to express yourself—including your anger—as a child and you were emotionally crushed for it.

That was certainly Junie's experience. She was ten years younger than her next older sister. She'd been a "surprise," her parents had said, and they were tired of raising kids. Every rebellion, every attempt to express herself, was met with rigidity, criticism, and a complete frustration of any conversation. Junie learned quickly that "the tall blade of grass gets mowed down" and became as outwardly compliant as she became filled with feelings of inadequacy and repressed rage.

Step 2. See the Story's Cost

Junie would do anything to avoid proving the fear in her story true. Yet it was precisely her story—the one that says she's insufficient and deserving of punishment—that has forced her into a role that guaranteed she would be less than she could be (indeed, with the anorexia, she wanted to extinguish herself completely). It was her fear, expressed through her story, that made her into someone she wasn't—into someone unreal.

By staying in her marriage (and therefore committing herself to being *less* than she could be as an adult), Junie tried to show herself and the world (and her mother and her father) that she's enough. Yet all the actions she took led her away step by step from being real and more deeply into her story of not being "enough."

When I point this out, Junie tilts her head and looks at me blankly. Then understanding set in and she shakes her head amazed. "Do you mean that everything I am doing to hold on to Andrew I'm doing so he won't leave me and show me and the world that I'm just not good enough to hold on to a man—that I expect to be punished so I encourage it? You're telling me that I am part of this, too. That I've been willing to trade who I can be, trade *myself* for this false proof!" Junie flushes with excitement. "Whoa, this blows my mind."

Like Junie, if you are a Self-defeater, your story will tell you to deny yourself in order to feel safe. When you do want good things, anxiety kicks in, warning you to stay away from "selfishness" because if you are selfish, you will be punished. Needless to say, after a while, Self-defeaters stop reaching for anything that might make them feel cared for or satisfied. In relationships, your habit of self-denial often provokes those close to you to act in kind. At work, you are the martyrs who ultimately don't succeed because your self-debasing behavior almost begs people to treat you badly. Your guilt about your own desires creates eating disorders and poor health and leaves you a great candidate for substance abuse. If you can see that you have actually played a hand in instigating these situations and take some responsibility for them, then you can see how your story has robbed you of direct, appropriate relationships in all areas of your life. Try to be aware of the losses—the loss of time, of people in your past, of your own personal identities—and grieve them. Because that is the only way you can give up strong feelings of revenge for past injuries that you are taking out on yourself.

Step 3. Rewrite Your Story

As a Self-defeater you have to replace your old story of not being worthy of love or happiness with this one: *"I want pleasure in life. I want to be able to trust others to like me as I am."* That means trusting that people will still love you if you get angry and express it directly. Your new story says that it's okay to be angry: *"I will express anger. I will be assertive. I will go out and get pleasure, and I will express and accept love."*

You have to tell yourself that you will not victimize yourself anymore. This will, in turn, stop provoking others to victimize you in kind. Rewriting your story means taking responsibility for your actions, not playing the martyr, and expressing yourself directly.

For Junie, rewriting her story meant she was going to have to see who she truly was and acknowledge what she was capable of doing, being, and feeling as an adult. If your story has been, like Junie's, that you aren't enough and you have to be a doormat in order to stay attached to a source of love, you have to become familiar with all the ways and times you lie down and let people walk all over you. Each time you see yourself heading for the floor, stop, and say something else—something like this instead: *"I am deserving of love and respect. I will ask to be treated as I would treat someone else, and I will not expect to be treated badly but rather encourage better for myself. If he leaves me because of that, I will find someone who loves me for who I really am."*

What would change in Junie's life if this was her story's message? Just about everything. It would give her marriage a fighting chance as she stood up for herself with Andrew. Andrew, too, would be forced to see that he had a true partner he couldn't ride roughshod over. Instead of wasting away in her dangerous anorexia, she would be healthy and strong and a better mother for her son. And finally, instead of making Andrew aware of her anger at him by her obvious silent suffering (which Andrew interpreted as constant criticism), she'd be able to express that anger directly instead of through the highly enraging habit of sighing all the time. The immediate benefit of that is that Andrew, the Superachiever that he is, would feel more adequate and she would feel more empowered, and they both could get down to the business of helping their son.

Step 4. Take New Actions

Guilt and anxiety push Self-defeaters back into old behaviors. So, the first new action for you means learning to recognize when you're feeling guilty or anxious and to not let those feelings stop you from breaking old patterns and trying new behaviors. Some of that means stopping your complaining, your subservient attitude, your slowness to help others, or your tendency to thwart others' wishes (all behaviors that make people want to victimize you!). More than anything else, it means not doing those things that make other people pick on you.

Junie had to make the decision to *use* her grown-up, real story. She had to stop reacting to Andrew in an automatic way that created the same old patterns, and she had to stop making the same old choices. Junie had to stop enabling Andrew's criticisms, which she did through her wounded silences. Her old story told her to blame herself for every one of Andrew's accusations and to play the willing victim. Now Junie decided that with her new story she'd see Andrew's superiority as *his* problem and would say to herself, "Okay, I've been here before. Here's the old story; here's what I would automatically do. I'd apologize madly—anything not to have him angry with me since he might leave me!" I asked Junie to make a list of new actions resulting from her new story's message: *"I am deserving of love and respect. I am not a bad person, deserving of punishment. I will ask to be treated as I would treat someone else, and I will not expect to be treated badly but rather encourage better for myself."* Here are a few items on her list:

- I will not give Andrew the suffering silent treatment anymore; instead, I'll put my sighs into words when I dislike his actions.
- When I am angry, I will say, "You're really crossing the line with me. I really want to be married to you, but this constant criticism is too much."
- I will not be a doormat.
- I will do something to have fun once a day.
- I will practice asking for something I want or need.

These new actions are all built around what a Self-defeater needs most—to know that it's safe to express emotions and needs. If one of your new actions carries a threat of real punishment with it—don't do it. There's a difference between losing weight you've gained and becoming anorexic—you can easily take a new action and turn it in against yourself because your old story will try to tell you that doing something in your own interest makes you a "bad" person. That's just your old story talking. Remember, you are deserving of love, attention, and self-expression, and the more you act on that new foundation, the sooner you will overcome your Self-defeater story.

Chapter Eleven

DEFEATING THE COMPETITOR STORY

If you are a Competitor (and this personality type is predominantly female), you first need to understand that most of the time you live in a no-win world. Whether or not you can admit it to yourself, many of your behaviors are motivated by your need for men's approval to feel complete, but at the same time, you feel guilty about being the object of their attention. You crave the love of women but feel angry with them for abandoning you to the men or for not liking you because men do. For you to overcome your story, you have to decide you're going to be able to tolerate some bad feelings in order to experience more genuine emotions. But the feelings of shame or guilt or self-loathing that might arise will be more than compensated for by the tremendous relief and fulfillment you'll get as a result of rewriting your story.

This certainly applied to Ann, who came to see me shortly after making a fool of herself at her younger sister's wedding. She'd had a bit too much to drink, and she'd made a very obvious pass at the best man, groping him in front of his date, who later stormed out of the reception. This caused a huge scene, but Ann wasn't aware of it because she was off dancing seductively with this young man.

Ann discovered how angry everyone was at her when she appeared hungover at breakfast the next morning, still stinging with mortification that the man next to her in the bed didn't even remember her name. As she joined her family in the hotel dining room, she sat down to stares of disapproval and disgust from her mother and her female cousins. Her father appeared oblivious to everything, but then again, he probably had a bit of a hurting head, too.

Ann started to get angry, blaming her mother for her behavior—after all, it was she who kept criticizing her about her weight, her clothes, her behavior. She recalled the disapproval on her mother's face at one point during the wedding as she watched Ann on the dance floor. Ann was always too wild for her mother's taste. Ann felt furious with her mother because she knew full well why she had no date for the wedding. Her biggest relationship was on again and off again with her significantly older, married boss. "But he's your father's age," her mother had sniffed when Ann wanted to invite him to the wedding. "I don't think it would be appropriate."

Growing up, Ann's only real solace was the way her father doted on her, and it wasn't too surprising to me that she acted out at her younger sister's wedding. She was in a constant competition with her for her father's affection, and what better time to show she was the sexiest, prettiest woman than on her little sister's big day? Her mother, a real "society" lady, had too many rules for Ann, and she could never measure up to her expectations. But her father always seemed to appreciate her. Even though she can't recall exactly what it was, something in her relationship with him validated her even as it made her feel something wasn't quite right. There was no abuse, but the boundaries weren't healthy ones. Her mother's rejection and her father's heightened interest in her and her sex life set her off on a path that left her very male-oriented. She blames herself, though, for not having an appropriate relationship. She fears she must be damaged somehow and that that's why she's not had a real relationship though she's rounding the bend toward the age of forty-one. Most of her relationships have been with married men or men who are so much older that there's no future in the relationships. The age didn't matter anyway, because the unions never lasted too long. Ann knows that if she were just thinner, prettier, and a little more ladylike—in other words, if she were like her sister—she'd have been dancing at her own wedding.

If Ann is going to rewrite her story, she has to realize that these men she chooses are stand-ins for her father, and she is stuck trying to possess him. She's going to have to look for someone at her level with whom she can have a real and loving partnership and not just a conquest. She's going to have to take a good look in the mirror and acknowledge that she wears short skirts and bold lipstick and push-up Wonderbras, and that this is very provocative behavior. *She's* the one not letting people see through to the real her—a woman who can be up and down, who can be soft and sweet and scared. She's going to have to stop distracting people with her sexuality and start letting those vulnerable, human parts of her be seen. She has to experience that she can be loved and valued for more than her sexuality.

Step 1. Tell Yourself Your Old Story

It's been hard for Ann to see her vulnerabilities herself or to stay with someone long enough for him to see them. Her Competitor story puts her in a vice grip—her actions express both a longing for and a dependency on men, but at the same time she feels resentful toward them. She has given men a tremendous amount of power. In her world, they are all-consuming gods—but harmful ones. "I am nothing without a man," her story goes. "I need gratification from men but their attention makes me feel guilty." If you are a Competitor, you experience tremendous inner conflict about your sexuality, about your relationships with women, and about what men really want from you. That makes it hard for you to see what you must—that your tantalizing behavior, your competitiveness, your wild and attention-getting emotional swings all dig you more deeply into your old story's plot that tells you you're nothing without a man and that you must compete with everyone for a man's attention. Because you have to acknowledge this and realize that you've been participating in behavior that makes you feel ashamed of yourself or embarrassed, it's hard to look at your old story.

As painful as it may be, close your eyes and think of a conflict in which you've been competitive with another woman. It may take some time to come up with an example because you've behaved out of need rather than out of desire—you've needed to "win" to feel powerful and to punish women for not saving you from men. Please try to empathize with yourself, though. You must understand that there is a tremendous amount of sadness and grief in your story because it's one that has left you feeling exploited and abandoned.

It takes Ann a few minutes to locate her current conflict even though it's obvious to me that it was her sister's wedding. Shame and guilt can cloud your eyes in this story. But soon, she settles in to discuss the events of that evening and admits to feeling guilt, shame, and embarrassment. She's also pissed off with both her perfect sister and her mother. But most of all, she's mad at the men—if only they could look beyond her boobs and the promise of sex. She's angry because she feels she's in a lose-lose situation because of her old story's message—either she's nothing without a man or if she gets one, she feels, in her words, "like crap."

Step 2. See the Story's Cost

To be free of the old story, Ann has to see that it has stained all her relationships and robbed her of love. It leaves her with tremendous guilt for inducing gratification from men's love and for the estrangement and distance from the affection of women. She's paid a heavy price: She is extremely lonely inside and feels misunderstood by the world. She feels men only want sex from her and women hate her for it. But inside, she knows there is more to the story. Acting according to the old story's plot keeps her from taking the risk of presenting herself to the world as more than a sexual being.

If you're a Competitor, one of the other huge costs of your story is that you rarely feel that anyone sees your accomplishments. You feel men only recognize your work because you're a woman and they want to have sex with you. You feel women belittle your achievements by saying any success you had was due to your looks or male-oriented behavior and not your work. You're furious with your parents for creating this situation—after all, you are the victim here. Thus, your story denies you any true satisfaction.

What has your story cost you? Can you see how it's led you to emphasize your sexuality? Can you see how it's made you minimize your other attributes and strengths? Your story leaves you with no self-worth, tons of guilt, and no real enjoyment of your sexuality. Take a good look at the times in your life when you have felt marginalized by women—at school, at camp, at home. How did you respond? And what price did you pay?

Step 3. Rewrite Your Story

Keeping in mind that your old story told you that you are nothing without a man, what happens when you turn that story inside out? Try substituting this message: *"I am full and complete as I am. I am responsible for my own actions and can control how I behave."* You have to change your story so that you don't see all men and women as either fantastic or evil but as a mixture of both. You then will be able to accept that everyone has sexual feelings and aggressive feelings and competitive feelings and loving feelings. Amazing changes happen when you rewrite your story to give you the message: *"I am lovable without flirting. I can have what I want without manipulation. I don't have to feel exploited. Women are not my enemies, and men are not my saviors. All women are not my mother, and all men are not my father. I deserve honest relationships with both sexes."*

Undoubtedly, at first, you will likely experience some depression as you begin rewriting your story. For a long time you've maintained the facade of "Oh, this is so great! I get one man after another, and who needs these women?" But once you look behind that bravado, you will see that you've been quite sad, and you may have to experience those emotions as you start on your new life.

You will also have to give up some of your identity. In your old story, you've played the dual role of the naive child and the evil seductress. In fact, you're neither the good girl nor the bad woman. You are neither horribly irresponsible nor purely guilty. You're not helpless around men, or so controlling and critical that you essentially castrate them. You're somewhere in the middle. You have to see that you've created those polarized identities as a key part of your story, and you've spent most of your time bouncing back and forth between the extremes. When you rewrite your story, you'll see that you've suffered great difficulty in your past, but you don't have to keep reliving it. Your new story gives you the right to be a woman who can receive *true* love and who can give real love irrespective of whether you've "won" a man from someone else. Your new story tells you that you're entitled to the love and relationship and not just the conquest.

Ann starts to cry quietly as she substitutes her new story's message. It's almost overwhelming because she experiences such a huge relief from shame. But she starts to get angry with her father and mother for creating the mess. I ask her to consider that one of the messages of her new story is that she is no one's easily manipulated plaything but instead is responsible for her own actions. At first Ann sputters, "But, but . . ." Then it starts to dawn on her that if the new message is true—and it will take some time to sink in—she won't feel exploited ever again. She sits quietly with this information.

Ann is beginning to see that her new story tells her that she can now—possibly—have a relationship with a man who wants a woman who has something to say and to give, a man who doesn't measure her by her nose or boobs. She doesn't have to take men from other women to feel adequate or to punish anyone. If she can be with men who don't have other women, she can have love without feeling so guilty.

Step 4. Take New Actions

For Ann to change and for her new story to take root, she has to metaphorically throw away the bustier and garter belt. She has to act like a woman among women. Constant flirting? Out. Putting other women down in front of men? Forget it. Manipulating? Not in the new world. Reach out to women. I ask her to put her new story in her consciousness and give me a few actions she could take based on it. Here are a few of them:

- Make a date for coffee with a woman with no agenda other than wanting her company.
- Take a break from dating for a while so I can get a sense of myself and what pleases me, not just men.
- Break off the affair with my married lover.
- Set some comfortable boundaries with my father.
- Go to work without wearing makeup—well, maybe go to the store without wearing makeup first . . .
- Spend some time with my mother—alone.

Now, you make a list. If you aren't ready to do some of those things—fine. This is a big change in perspective, and you may have to take baby steps at first. Become aware of what you do every day in your appearance that starts up and reinforces the old story and do something differently.

If you are married or in a relationship, keep your eyes peeled for any behavior where you use your femininity to get what you want. Anything that derives from those behaviors is tainted fool's gold.

Authentic relationships come from rewriting the Competitor story. Ann had been hidden in her old story and therefore could never have a real relationship with any man. The road to "real" for Ann means owning up to the fact that sleeping with the best man at her sister's wedding was not a random event. She must admit she's been on a continual quest to steal men away from other women, and that it's her behavior that has led to her loneliness more so than the fifteen extra pounds or her mother, who she's blamed all these years.

When you overcome your Competitor story, huge gifts arrive. The first is that you can have meaningful relationships—with men *and* women. Because you both presented and resented the sexy shell you showed to the world, when you climb out of it, besides feeling vulnerable you will expose all your other wonderful attributes that aren't encased in seductive behavior. People will see—*you will see*—the multifaceted person you are, and your life will become rich and full. Everything will stop feeling so conditional on your looks, and you will feel a growing measure of self-confidence and emotional security as you let people see your entire humanity. This leads to intimacy and recognition—the two things you most desire and deserve.

Chapter Twelve

DEFEATING THE PERFECTIONIST STORY

Tolerance and flexibility are the new story themes for the Perfectionist. Perfectionists need tolerance for their own frailties and the overwhelming sense of anxiety any imperfection causes as well as flexibility for other's imperfections. I want Emily to understand this because she needs some serious guidance right away. Her teenage daughter, Julie, has completely shut her out, and she fears her husband, Gary, is having an affair. He's had it with her rigid ways, he says, and the evening before our appointment, he'd slammed out of the house yelling, "Sorry, Em, but I didn't get the rule book when we got married. Since you know the right way to do everything, why don't you just do it yourself?" He hadn't come home. Julie had watched the entire incident and had shut her bedroom door on Emily when she'd tried to talk to her about the fight. Not a word had come from Julie's room, and uncharacteristically she was gone before Emily woke up the next morning. It was beginning to dawn on Emily that Gary may not have been the only one who'd not slept at home last night.

This was not how it was supposed to be. All she did was tell Gary that he had to send a present to his boss's daughter for her confirmation. That was what was done. She hadn't wanted him to pay a consequence for ignoring what was proper. "But we weren't invited to the party!" Gary countered.

"It doesn't matter," Emily had responded. "*You* should do what's right even if the other person doesn't." That was all it had taken to send him flying from the house.

"I called my mother," she said. "She understood completely. I mean, there's a right way and a wrong way, right? And you do what's right."

Of course Emily's mother reinforced Emily's dictates. She'd installed them. Perfectionists beget Perfectionists more often than not. Right and wrong. Proper and improper. Moral and immoral. Living in a highly rigid, black-and-white world creates children who feel completely insecure if they don't then re-create that world themselves. Gary's flexibility and Julie's adolescent rebellions threatened Emily on a level none of them could appreciate—until now. Emily was beginning to see that the problems might lie with her worldview more than with her family's.

Perfectionists have so little wiggle room, so little space for making mistakes. They live with a constant need to control everyone and everything. Rewriting their stories means relinquishing some of that control—and doing this makes them extremely agitated and anxious. But they gain a tremendous feeling of safety in return—after they see that their way is not the only way and that many roads can lead them safely to where they want to go.

For Emily to overcome her story, it's going to take some hard work on her part. She lives in such a state of moral judgment that it's going to be hard for her to even contemplate relaxing her standards. They are, after all, all that keep her world contained and free from total chaos, leading to the abandonments she is now experiencing anyway. She is going to have to put herself in her current conflict and reach back through her memory to see that inflexibility sits at the heart of most of her conflicts in life. I ask her to sit in the feelings last night's fight brought up without jumping to any rationalizations or without blaming her husband or daughter.

If Emily can just develop some compassion for herself (not a strong suit in Perfectionists as it seems morally weak to many), she can see that her need for rules and for right and wrong comes from her earliest days when she was taught to adhere to what was right outside her rather than what she felt was right inside her. Overcoming the Perfectionist story means broadening everything—the possibility that others can be right, that there's more than one way to do things, that life is multifaceted, textured, and complex in the best of ways. The world will get so much bigger and richer for Emily if she can just trust herself enough to know that loosening up doesn't equal abandoning herself to destruction.

Step 1. Tell Yourself Your Old Story

In the Perfectionist story, there is a rule for everything, and it must be followed or else . . . It's easy to spot the story in action. If "my way or the highway" is the background tune playing, you're in your old story. If you feel rigid, inflexible, and very sure that you are right, you are in the Perfectionist story. But be gentle. Dismantling these very hard-and-fast rules about the way things should and must be creates chaos inside. Take it slowly; take it compassionately. Remember that the Perfectionist is like the person who swims across a lake with a rock in her hand. When she starts to drown under its weight, people yell from the shore, "Drop the rock!" And as she slowly sinks into the depths, she answers "I can't—it's mine."

I ask Emily to try to identify herself as a person who needs order all the time. It's important that she recognize her history so she can empathize with her story's origins. In Emily's case, there was no traumatic past, just a highly codified society of manners, morals, and homogeneity. In her small town in southern Illinois, how to do things was clear.

But when Emily had gone to college in Ann Arbor, Michigan, in the 1980s, life was anything but orderly. That's one of the reasons she'd married Gary so quickly upon graduation—he'd come from a similar background; he understood her. It made sense. But under his surface manners beat a very different heart—one that was so unruly in itself that he craved the structure Emily brought to his life. As Emily looks at their symbiosis, she starts to see why they needed each other as much as they did and why, as time went on and Gary's disorderly emotionality became more evident, her response was to become ever more vigilantly structured.

I ask Emily if she can tell me what she believes about her life. "That there's a right way and a wrong way to do things," she says. "That we need rules for a civilized society. That I am teaching my daughter rules to live by, and even if she doesn't appreciate them now, she will later. Kids need firm guidelines; otherwise they get all messed up." When I ask how she uses these rules in her life, Emily responds, "They're what make me effective at work. They make me a good, predictable manager. People appreciate knowing exactly what's expected of them." This may or may not be true—I can't evaluate her statement. But it does show me that Emily's Perfectionist personality infuses every aspect of her life.

I try to get her to go back to her earliest memories so that she can see she's been following the orders of an old story. Emily remembers a time when she was in elementary school when her mother's brother— her favorite uncle—announced that his wife had left him and he was getting a divorce. Her mother had been horrified. Instead of comforting her brother, she'd read him the riot act. "What did you do?" she'd accused. "No one in this family has ever gotten divorced. Marriage is a sacrament. I'm appalled." Emily watched as a tear slid from her uncle's eye. She longed to rush up and hug him but feared her mother's response. As she loaded the dinner dishes into the dishwasher, she heard the front door open and close. She hadn't seen her uncle again until her wedding day. Emily clearly saw the consequences of violating established order. And she began to recognize how, in the absence of any other role models, she also had embraced the need to cling to a highly ordered world—no matter the human cost.

Step 2. See the Story's Cost

Living the Perfectionist story means blocking out or obliterating anything that doesn't meet the story's exacting standards—as Gary and Julie had experienced on many occasions. So many people and so many adventures are exiled this way. So much of life's whimsy, originality, and surprise is rejected. These stories make for very small lives sometimes. The walls that keep things out will trap you in if you're a Perfectionist. That's why you often feel so rejected and misunderstood but also irritated by those who just don't understand or don't know better. You may have felt like you weren't the most popular person on the block, but, on the other hand, if you're really honest with yourself, there might be some measure of pride in that—who would want to be liked by *those* people anyway? Well, in truth, you would.

Emily admits she's got very few friends—it's part of the reason she entered treatment with me in the first place. Normally, she wouldn't have sought out therapy—no one in her family had ever gone before. But she couldn't tell her mother about what was going on in her home life, and she had no good friend she really trusted. Most of her relationships were much more formal than what she needed right now. She does see that her attitude toward people has made her, as she says, "an island unto myself." She knows she needs help in her marriage and is beginning to see that she holds some responsibility for the mess things are in. Likewise, she sees that her strict ethical codes of behavior have really alienated her daughter. She's ready to change rather than lose the two people she really loves. It's just that she has no clue how.

Step 3. Rewrite Your Story

Emily knows her old story's message—she finds herself consciously either saying it or thinking it several times a day: "There's a right way and a wrong way, and your way is wrong." I suggest she substitute a new one that goes like this: *"There's no right or wrong—I can make a mistake and so can the people around me. I can be flexible and tolerant, and my life will expand and deepen with each new open-minded experience."*

This seems like a huge leap for Emily, and it probably is. She's going to have to sneak up on this new life slowly; otherwise she might go skittering back to the safety of her more enclosed life. But if you are a Perfectionist, your new story is going to bring tremendous liberation. In this real version of life, you and the people around you are allowed to have personal preferences of things you would actually *like* to do, not just feel you *have* to do.

After being rule-bound for so many years, this new freedom is sure to be disorienting. It also asks you to let life get a little messy, even faulty. Beds can remain unmade, thank-you notes unwritten. The "authority" figure in your life can stop being worshiped. "I have opinions of my own," the new story says. "I may not do it right, but I can try something new." These statements were previously unimaginable.

"I can like who I want—or not! I can do what I like—or not!" Such incredible choices! Don't be surprised, however, if the new story creates tremendous anxiety at first, because the authority figure—whether present or internalized—is toppling, and this may lead to feelings of lack of safety. You may also find that you become extremely self-critical. Try to be empathic. Remember that this story started out of a profound need for emotional security and predictability in a world that felt terribly threatening. So be kind and gentle and don't beat yourself up. Just because new behavior feels awkward and unnatural doesn't mean it's "wrong." Finally, don't be surprised if you feel a little disoriented. With no one to please, with no one to whom your devotion can be demonstrated, there are no immediate compass points leading you down the new path. You've been accustomed to being motivated by what's right, not by what's pleasurable. But hang in there because step by step with each new choice, with each new preference, your prison door will creak open a little more.

Step 4. Take New Actions

This is going to be the tough part for you. Because Perfectionists experience a high level of discomfort when they learn that the world is much richer and bigger than imagined, things can get pretty tense at first. Learning relaxation methods—breathing exercises, yoga, taking walks—will help you get a handle on the high emotions that result from new freedom. Have you ever stood in a doorway with your arms pressing out on the frames? When you step away, your arms feel light and float up. The new steps in a Perfectionist's life can feel this weightless—that is why new actions need to be taken gently and patiently.

Because you haven't exactly been "the life of the party," learning to teach yourself how to be warmer to other people is an excellent first step. Whether you realized it or not, your rigidity toward people often made you appear judgmental to others when you felt they were "errant" or "mistaken." What goes around comes around, as they say, and you're going to find that it takes a while for people to realize you have changed.

Expressing warmth, expressing loving feelings, and expressing anger—all of which you've found it difficult to do—are all new actions that come directly out of your new story's message.

Letting it be okay to get messy and make mistakes also makes the list. You must learn to tolerate—even to celebrate—more imperfection in yourself and in others. But to do that you're going to have to relinquish some control over yourself and others and make concerted efforts to "go with the flow."

Of course, these kind of actions were hardly going to be easy for Emily. The fact that Emily doesn't believe in mistakes hasn't saved her from making any. In fact, she's made quite a few—her rigidity and inflexibility have cost her a good marriage, and she's about to really damage her relationship with her daughter if she doesn't lighten up.

Emily does understand intellectually that her daughter is a teenager and therefore a complete jumble inside. I tell her that she doesn't have to like what's going on, but she has to work on accepting it or pay a very high price. I tell her to try to use humor—a stunning suggestion to the usually too serious Perfectionist. I suggest she might get Julie to clean her room if she gives Julie a potted plant and jokingly tells her it might take root in her pile of dirty clothing. I suggest almost anything to get Emily to stop being so rigid, because her constant need to be right is making them both miserable.

"I guess I have to put some trust in her that she'll be okay if I don't tell her every last thing, huh?" Emily says with a sigh. "Exactly," I tell her. "Hands off. Let her make her own mistakes. Otherwise, you'll keep her a baby—and an angry one at that." I then ask her what other new actions she can take. Here's some of what was on her list:

- I can make a mistake and tell my daughter about it.
- I can tell Gary that I'm struggling with not knowing how to do this marriage "right."
- I can let my daughter do whatever she wants in her room as long as it's hygienic.
- I will make a call to a woman friend for no reason other than to ask for her company.
- I will stop dividing up the world into black or white.

Once Emily gets going, she doesn't stop—indeed, she's trying to do it perfectly! But she laughs when I point that out. There's proof that she's conscious of her old story and is already starting to overcome it!

Emily tries awkwardly to let things go—it doesn't come easily to her. But slowly, Julie has come to an understanding. Julie sees that her mother has "issues," as she says, around this "little miss perfect" thing. Gradually, I believe that if Emily can keep telling herself her new story—that she can let go and the world will be safe and that others will be fine—she will have a richer and fuller relationship with her daughter.

I'm not so sanguine about her life with Gary. It will take a patient man to hang in with her as she inwardly rolls a critical eye at his "mistakes." The questions for her are, Can she live with someone's faults if he turns me on? Can I really let someone love me when I'm incorrect? Can I really let myself love someone not perfect themselves? This was a woman who once dumped a man for picking "tacky" floor tiles. But the desire for an authentic relationship in which she is seen for who and what she is motivates Emily. She wants to feel rooted in her love and her life—not in her rule book.

As with all Perfectionists, Emily's old story forced her to carry the weight of the world on her shoulders. Her new story will be one of compromise, of fifty-fifty, of give-and-take, and of learning to love a flawed self. It will be a new story of old adages—rules are made to be broken and life is messy—but with each new misstep or broken rule, the load will lighten every day.

Rewriting our stories creates a powerful choice for all of us—we can revert to our old stories or step into new ones. We can slip and err and regress. But if we keep our new messages close at hand, if we make the decision to be conscious of them, we will find the ultimate reward of textured and full lives—authentic and real.

Chapter Thirteen

TEN ROADBLOCKS TO AUTHENTICITY

Our old stories are like dogs protecting a bone—they don't give up without a fight. When we start digging around in our old stories, exposing them to the light of our adult consciousness, we also bring up old hurts. We necessarily revisit the original conflicts or situations that caused us to create the stories in the first place to overcome them. Not surprisingly, our unconscious minds spring to their rescue and employ a variety of defense mechanisms to thwart any examination or change by denying and distracting and projecting our problems onto others.

Everyone has defenses. They exist to guard our characters and our stories. Much of what we say or do comes from them. They may help us avoid pain, but they do so at the expense of keeping our myths in place. They are there to make us feel safe. But they are roadblocks to real change and authenticity, because even as they protect us, their purpose is to lock in old behaviors—ones that worked when we were small but that ultimately block our paths as we grow. We need to learn to spot our defenses and know when we're in a defensive state if we want to overcome our stories.

Defenses have many positive qualities. They keep us from being overwhelmed—mostly by anxiety. They allow us to deal with inappropriate instinctual urges or overpowering environmental demands. Without them, we couldn't function. If Americans weren't able to emotionally defend themselves the day after 9/11, no one would have been able to leave their homes. Defenses help us to carry on in the midst of tragedy by creating an alternative version of what has happened. Think about what happens when we mourn something: We go through the famous five stages of grief—denial, anger, bargaining, depression, and acceptance. These emotions keep us from confronting our losses head-on until we are emotionally ready to absorb and accept them.

But defenses also prohibit our personalities from changing. Because of the way they work, they make others wrong and keep us right. They shift the focus away from what threatens or hurts. By doing so, they allay the anxiety that we feel whenever our personalities are "attacked." But this protection comes at a price—by avoiding situations that could lead us to self-examination and change, defensive behaviors seal in the childish emotions that sit in the center of our stories and keep us from becoming fully realized adults.

When we deal with products of the unconscious, we can't face them directly. When patients first come into my office, I can't say, "Gee, you have a story and this is what it is." First, I don't know what their stories are right off the bat, and, second, the most natural response to that sentence would be to deny it utterly and thus block any help. Denial is one of the most common defenses, and when it's present it's impossible to make meaningful changes. Thus, when trying to understand our defenses, we have to be patient and watchful.

Each of the ten most common defenses, or roadblocks, creates certain clear behaviors. They reveal themselves in layers, and when we confront one, we tend to panic and scramble instinctually to the safety of another defense. The key is to peel them away a little bit at a time and, as we do, slowly reveal the vulnerable child they defend. When we become aware of a defense, it loses its power. As adults, we have the opportunity to revisit our pasts, assess what happened, and adjust our messages to suit our mature abilities. But we can't do that until we learn to spot and defuse our defenses.

The Role of Anxiety

Anxiety is the lion guarding the gate of change. It lies in wait ready to spring whenever something in our lives reminds us of our original conflicts, thus triggering the feelings of old hurts or unfulfilled desires. Anxiety is a feeling of fear from some perceived threat. The threat can be internal or external. You'll feel anxiety if you are standing in the middle of the road and a car is coming. Anxiety's purpose is very important because it's an alert that something's wrong. For instance, if you're on a date and the guy says, "Let's go back to my place" and you hardly know him, you get anxious. The anxiety may be telling you that it's not a good idea to go with him because something bad could happen. That's anxiety's positive role—a warning signal that protects you.

But then there's the other kind of anxiety—the kind that wakes you up at four in the morning worried about all the things you have to do.

Under that anxiety sits the threat that you aren't good enough or you are going to lose your job or husband or that people won't look up to you and respect you. Under that anxiety sits the feeling you are a failure. No wonder anxiety jump-starts our defenses. Who can sit with those awful feelings?

Feeling anxious is terrible. When we get that jumpy feeling and nothing sits right, our attention shortens and we get snappish. We feel like there is something we should be doing to feel calmer, but we just can't figure out what it is. So we act. We do something to discharge the nervous feelings. We do whatever it is we learned to do as kids to resolve the anxiety. We go silent or eat or fight or spend or work or make alibis or exercise. We do whatever we can to calm that agitation that crawls around just under our skins. We deploy our defenses.

When we want to know if we are being real or not, anxiety is a real clue for us because it's the story's starting point. We may not be aware of the unconscious, but we can begin to know that anxiety is its guardian. When we feel anxious, it's a pretty good bet that unless we do something differently, we are going to start doing whatever it is we've done all our lives to resolve the inner conflicts that cause the anxiety in the first place.

Everybody gets anxious. Everybody has a different way of dealing with the anxiety that comes up when we have an inner impulse or wish to do something that some other part of us considers unacceptable. When we have a day off and want to just laze around but know we really should focus on our tax preparation, we become anxious. We get caught between the desire to indulge ourselves ("I don't feel like working. I just want to have fun!") and the need to use our time productively ("It's good to work. It's bad to slack off!").

If we're a few pounds overweight when we go to see our mothers, we fear they're going to point out how tightly our jeans fit (which translates into "we are not good enough" or "not acceptable" when we remember it's a little kid inside who is receiving these messages). We want to be with our mothers and want to yell at them, too. But if we push away the ones we love, who will love us? Those feelings create conflict, and that conflict creates anxiety.

Anxiety has a very sensitive volume control—it can go from a whisper to a shout in seconds. As we start to consciously link its presence to its source, we can begin the process of change and start off down the path of authenticity. I can tell you, however, that nothing makes us more edgy than the idea of changing our personalities and threatening our emotional security blankets—after all, so much of our identities and lives rests on this foundation. So it's critical to understand and learn to recognize the ten defenses initiated by anxiety that guard against all inquiries. When we learn to spot these roadblocks, they lose their power to alter reality, and though momentarily deterred from our progress toward being real, we can look at each one with compassion—after all, they're only doing their jobs! It's just that we just don't need them anymore.

The Ten Roadblocks to Progress

1. Denial

Karen swore she would never get divorced. Her parents had separated quite unpleasantly when she was four, and although her memories were dim, she knew that the fallout from the dissolution had spread out over the years, poisoning both her parents. As a consequence, Karen—a Dependent—almost didn't get married at all, but in her late thirties, she fell in love with a coworker, married, and had a child all within a year.

Everything was wonderful for the first year. She and her husband were very excited by her growing belly. Richard had a heavy travel schedule but cut it way back as Karen neared her ninth month. Their baby, Joshua, arrived midsummer. Karen found that caring for him absorbed most of her attention and time. Besides, Richard had started traveling again—so much that he logged more than 100,000 miles that first year traveling back and forth to Asia.

Karen missed Richard. Even when he was home, he felt increasingly absent. She watched the other dads in the park with their children. She wished Richard would take Joshua for walks. But he was either away or sleeping off the latest jet lag. Their sex life became nonexistent. When Richard was around, the television was on constantly. Karen found she had to ask to be kissed good night and even lowered herself to beg for sex. "Too tired," Richard told her. "You try doing what I do and see how aroused you get."

Karen resigned herself to this way of life and started defending Richard to her sister whenever she called. "He's in a depression, Nell," she would insist. "He feels trapped by this job." Karen skirted the issue of Richard's increasing invisibility.

Nell suspected something more than traveling was going on. "Do you think he could be having an affair?" she asked Karen.

Karen was dumbstruck by the suggestion. "Not possible," she said. "He works too hard for that. It's just that this round-the-world travel schedule has made him horribly depressed."

Having become increasingly concerned about Karen, Nell went to visit her just around Joshua's second birthday. Richard, who never liked Nell, had just returned from a trip to Brazil and was not happy to see her at the apartment. Sensing her presence wasn't desired, Nell tried to be helpful by doing the laundry in the basement of the building so her sister could have some time with her husband.

Then, Nell found it. A size-ten blue bikini bottom buried in Richard's clothes. "Travel indeed," she said weighing whether or not to tell Karen.

When Karen came down to help, Nell asked, "Is this yours?" She held up the bikini bottom.

"Never saw it before. Where'd you find it?" Karen asked, as it slowly dawned on her that it came from Richard's pile. "That could be anyone's," she said after a moment. "There are fifty apartments in this building. Someone probably just left it in the dryer by mistake." She proceeded to hang it over the community bulletin board where its presumed owner would find it, returned to folding laundry, and forgot about it.

Everybody uses "denial." It's the biggest roadblock of them all. You don't like what's going on? Simply deny it. It's such a powerful defense that we even deny death. An aura of unreality hangs around the loved ones of the immediately deceased—disbelief, an inability to absorb the truth. We need some denial so that we can let reality slowly sink in with traumatic situations. The process of mourning means alternating between thinking about something and accepting it one moment and saying, "No, this can't be so," the next moment.

Patients will use denial in psychoanalytic treatment. They need to face the facts slowly. This is part of why therapy can take so long, because when confronting painful truths or revisiting painful occurrences, it's human nature to vacillate back and forth between what really happened and what a person's version is of what happened.

As you confront your story, as you see something that at first you admit is true, don't be surprised if you're walking around a few hours later and saying to yourself, "What was I thinking? I feel criticized and hurt and I don't buy this B.S." All that means is your denial is present; it's holding your story in place. As you start to uncover things, you are probably going to wax and wane between a little denial and a little less denial. Don't beat yourself up, however; remember that denial is there to protect you. It's just doing its job so you don't get overwhelmed with negative thoughts like "I'm a miserable person."

2. Projection

Helen decided—against her husband's wishes—to pull their daughter, Hailey, out of public school and put her in the prestigious, if stuffy, Miss Alcott's all-girl's school for her fourth-grade year. Ned, her husband, had come from a background full of girls who had gone to the Miss Alcott's of the world and had run as fast and as far as he could from it. Settling far from Boston in eastern Wisconsin and marrying Helen, a nice "non-society" girl from Minnesota, had cemented his rebellion. Now she wanted to put their daughter right back in the social circle he found so suffocating. Worse, it reminded him of his own childhood—which wasn't a very good memory. More than anything, the decision surprised Ned. Helen had always been uncomfortable around his family and in his milieu. She felt she was always being judged and wasn't up to snuff. She, more than he, had been critical of the airs his mother and sisters put on. However, he had always secretly feared she loved him for his money and station as much as for his personality. Now this really made him wary.

"Helen," he objected, "that school is full of social climbers. Why do we want Hailey there?"

"I'm not like that," Helen rejoined. "I'm not doing this for social status."

"But everyone thinks they're such hot stuff. It's going to bring out the worst in Hailey. Not to mention you," he said, trying to remind her that she had never felt at ease in the country-club world.

"You just think I'm not good enough!" she yelled at him. "You have always felt I was inferior."

"I most certainly do not," Ned said clearly and without anger.

"Now you're furious with me!" Helen cried, causing Ned to shake his head in bafflement. "You know I hate it when you're mad at me and now you are! Just for wanting to help our kid have the best she can have."

That's projection. After her denial doesn't work, Helen projects her own worst fears about herself—that she's not good enough—onto Ned, who actually adores her just the way she is. All he was trying to do was save her from going somewhere she wouldn't feel comfortable. We've all heard that old saying, "When one finger points out, three fingers are pointing back." That's projection.

When you hear yourself saying, "That's them, not me," be on the lookout for this powerful defense. "Projection" attributes your own wish or thought or action to someone else. It's a slightly more sophisticated defense than denial, where we simply deny that the problem exists. When Helen's denial ("I'm not like that") fails, she proceeds to projection ("It's your idea; you don't think I'm good enough") rather than recognizing it's she who feels inadequate.

Helen is a Self-defeater. Always shadowed by feelings of not being enough, she had hoped, subconsciously, that by marrying Ned she would finally be accepted by the world. He was handsome, smart, rich, and connected. But it hadn't worked. She still felt inferior to everyone. Now she projects her deepest fears onto her daughter, Hailey.

Ned clearly sees Helen's weakness yet he loves her anyway. But she would be crushed if she were exposed as the insecure and indeed envious girl that she is. Her defenses mediate the truth. People can handle a certain amount of affect—by "affect" I mean depression, anxiety, guilt, fear. But when an emotion overwhelms the defense, very often people come to see someone like me.

Helen became very angry during the discussion with Ned but accused him of being the angry one. She projected onto him the very state of anger she had trouble tolerating herself. These are all protective mechanisms for dealing with feelings we can't manage or images of ourselves that cause pain.

3. Identification

"Identification" is more complex than the first two defenses. When we deploy this mechanism, what we do is "borrow" someone else's behavior as our own, thus allowing us to not have to face the reality of what we're doing. It's like being able to have an action without a consequence because we associate ourselves with others whose behaviors we approve of.

Identification is sneaky—it's very hard to spot. But if your facts don't line up with your fantasy, suspect this defense. Think about a time when you were having a meal with a very slender person. When dessert comes, suddenly you think, "If she can eat it so can I," even though you don't have the same metabolism. That's identification.

Ann, the woman who slept with the best man at her sister's wedding, was having an affair with the married boss at work. At the time, he was separated from his wife, so the affair wasn't "bad" in her mind. But even after they reconciled—he did have two little girls after all—

she let the affair linger on. When I point out that maybe this might not be such a good thing, Ann tells me, "Oh, I know. It's just incidental that he happened to be married. You know me—I would never do that intentionally [denial!]. But my friend Ellen got into the same situation, and she broke it off the minute her lover went back to his wife. Don't worry. I'm doing the same thing."

Remember that Ann is a Competitor, whose personality is built on successfully stealing men's attention away from their women. She defends herself from her own self-judgment and from what she suspects others think about her by using identification as her defense. She does this by denying her actions, detaching herself from something she feels is negative, and then associating herself with someone positive. She doesn't even realize that she's been holding on to "This isn't the real me—I'm like Ellen," in order to not examine her own life.

When Ann thinks of herself, she sees a really moral person like Ellen. And because Ellen wouldn't continue an affair with a married man, Ann wouldn't either—despite the fact she was doing that very thing. I'm not saying this is consistent with reality because it's not— that's what defenses are all about. By equating herself with Ellen, Ann avoids examining her behavior, because if she did, she would come face-to-face with her old hurts from an overly interested and highly sexual father and a distant mother who never stood up for her.

4. Undoing

"Undoing" means doing or wishing some harmful wish and then fixing it somehow. Let's go back to Junie, the Self-defeater, and her husband, Andrew. Junie cannot directly express aggression—she's manifesting her anger with Andrew indirectly by telling their son to ignore his father's insistence on academic excellence. This has only served to increase Adam's anxiety—and Junie knows it on some level. But, in Junie's mind, she's arming her son to see "the truth" that being an A student isn't everything in life. "I'm helping him to see that life is bigger than just his accomplishments. He'll be better for it," she justifies. In her mind, she defends her behavior not only by taking away the consequence of her actions but also by "improving" the situation. She's done her son some real emotional harm by setting up a conflict between his parents, but she's undone that conflict by rationalizing that it will be better for her son.

Think of being at work and gossiping about your boss. Then you feel bad about it, so you go into her office all sweetness and light and ask how you can be more helpful. It may appear to be an attack of conscience, and perhaps it is. But more likely, if you're a Dependent, by saying catty things behind her back, you've created a distance between yourself and someone you feel you need badly. You urgently must undo this separation or face the feelings you have deep inside about being abandoned because you did something to deserve it. So you act sweet to reconnect and stave off the fear that not being nice will result in your abandonment.

5. Regression

"Regression" is when you revert to childlike behaviors—whether by becoming sick or incapacitated or unable to be a threat to someone else—your mother, your boss, or your friend. This happens all the time—you see adult women fighting with their mothers, and in the middle of the disagreement they say, "Oh, by the way, I've had these terrible headaches and stomachaches." They become helpless again so their mothers won't pick on them. Or they do things out in the world that make them seem like defenseless children. They lose their jobs or lose their relationships and regress. By returning to some earlier stage, they nullify any threat they might be to someone else and thus avoid having to take responsibility for their predicaments.

As Ann and I started making progress with rewriting her story, she told me she was sure she had mononucleosis. She was exhausted all the time. She couldn't make our sessions. She couldn't finish a critical project at work. She was going to take to her bed for a while and said she'd call me when she felt better. After she saw her doctor, as I had suggested, she came in to see me and said it hadn't been mono after all; she needed sleep. She'd tried to regress but once confronted with the proof she was telling herself a story, she picked herself up and continued to examine her actions and perform her responsibilities.

Not surprisingly, this defense is often found in Competitors. When you feel competitive and would like to eradicate your friend because she got the benefit chairwoman job that you didn't, you may regress and act as if you wouldn't have been good at it anyway. That way, you have no ability to challenge her—and you say so to her. That is a defense against the feeling you'd like to up the ante a million percent and ride roughshod over her and go tell the committee that they've made a huge mistake by entrusting her rather than you.

Instead, you say to her, "Could you please show me how you did that fund-raising appeal? I'm just so bad at it, and yours is so good." You act incompetent to compensate for your deeper hostile feelings.

6. Repression

"Repression" is when you truly put something into your unconscious mind, obliterating all conscious knowledge of something you should know. If you've been fighting with your mother, you might forget it's her birthday or Mother's Day. Your husband has been driving you nuts and you completely forget about the business cocktail party you're supposed to attend. When you do this, when you repress knowledge, you are defending yourself against the feelings of both loving and hating someone, and you are avoiding the conflict by "forgetting."

Often repression occurs when something traumatic happened at a young age. When you hear people say, "I don't remember anything of my childhood" or "I don't remember anything before I was eight," it's a real sign that something happened that was too overwhelming to be incorporated into their lives.

One afternoon as Sydney and I worked on her fears about marrying Brian, she suddenly became very pale. "Oh, my God," she whispered, "I just remembered something." Sydney had recalled that her father had once come back to the house. She had been home by herself; her mother had gone somewhere—she couldn't remember where. Her father clearly hadn't expected anyone to be home—Sydney figured she had been home sick from school that day or something. But the key had turned in the lock, and there was her father in the doorway. She had run to him, sure he was back to stay. He'd pushed her away and told her he was just there to pick up something and she should never tell her mother that he had been in the house. Sydney had watched him go to the desk in the living room and retrieve a piece of paper. On the way out, he'd hugged her with one arm. She never saw him again.

The promise of intimacy ripped away had bored deeply into Sydney's unconscious, and the incident was so painful she was all too willing to bury the entire incident and repress it.

Repressed memories can be very painful when they surface. And sometimes they can be unreliable, too. We distort things when we stuff them away, and it's best to check out some of these memories with either a trained mental health specialist or with someone who knows you and your life well before you take them as gospel. They are powerful tools but only when used safely.

As you begin to uncover your story, you may find that some memories are inaccessible. Be patient. They'll come when you feel emotionally secure enough to continue probing these painful, sensitive areas.

7. Isolation

By using "isolation," you remove uncomfortable or unbearable emotions and sequester them from your awareness. Say you publicly embarrassed a close friend over a slight infraction when you normally would have been patient. Rather than sit with your own feelings of remorse or regret about your behavior, you isolate those painful emotions and shift the focus to her misdeed, using it to rationalize your behavior. You would do this if the emotion that was involved—in this case, shame—was a particularly difficult feeling for you, one that brought up things from your past. So you avoid the consequential guilty feeling by compartmentalizing it and, in effect, boxing it up and putting it on a shelf.

8. Sublimation

"Sublimation" is when we turn a bad thought or feeling into a socially acceptable one. When a person feels mean or bad, rather than being aware of that unacceptable feeling, she will become the opposite on the outside of what she feels she is inside. Because it's so difficult to face feelings of anger, destruction, or rage, often these get sublimated into the helping professions where a desire to hurt becomes the will to protect. The disgust of the infirm becomes the call to caretaking.

Emily used sublimation as a real block to her progress. By profession, Emily was a social worker. She'd run the Head Start program in her county for the past three years. Whenever we would start to talk about her relationship with her daughter Julie, she would tell me a story about another family she'd helped at work. All this covered up the fact that she wasn't spending time with Julie. As a matter of fact, the more angry she became with Julie's rebellion, the more Emily sublimated it by proving to me and the world that she was a good, caring person.

This roadblock is a tough one if you're a Perfectionist because your outsides look great and moral and right. But if you are acting this way to cover up inner anger or aggression, it's like putting on a girdle and kidding yourself that you've actually lost your tummy.

9. Reaction Formation

Lisa, the Self-defeater with the terribly critical father, had gone back to work after her mother's death. We were working on rewriting her passive-aggressive story. In her new job, she had a very aggressive boss, who she'd quickly come to hate. He picked on the tiniest things— just as her father did—and drove her absolutely crazy. At work, she walked around seething with inner powerlessness and rage. The other day at lunch, she let it slip to a coworker—her boss's boss's executive assistant—that he hadn't done the research in a report that he said he had. A week later, her boss was reassigned to a more menial position. Rather than face her feelings directly, Lisa had caused another person to basically lose his job. But rather than look at the consequences of her old behavior, she used reaction formation and rationalized that she had actually saved him from the total humiliation he would have experienced had the truth come out in the press. Instead of facing that, she'd gotten him demoted.

Lisa will never get past her old story if she keeps behaving according to it and then covering up her behavior with a defense like this. When I point out that's what's happened, she denies it at first but then admits that her rage—expressed indirectly according to her old story—may have caused harm. In the end, the harm extended to Lisa, too, since she had to live with the guilt of what she'd done—which didn't help her self-esteem one bit.

"Reaction formation" allows you to keep a "bad" wish out of your awareness by focusing in on an opposite "good" wish. When you do this, you convince yourself that your motives are good. It's a relatively sophisticated defense but a total roadblock because it shifts all the responsibility from you to everyone else and keeps you from realizing that you can still make mistakes and be okay.

10. Humor

This final defense is the most sophisticated. It can be quite a positive one. I try to use "humor" with patients because it allows me to point out a defense in a nonthreatening way. By making light of a self-destructive defense, sometimes we can get to the heart of what patients are protecting, because if I do it humorously, they don't fear judgment.

On the other hand, it does have a dark side. So many entertainers use self-deprecating humor to put themselves down instead of facing the painful feelings inside. I can't tell you how many office jokes I get about thighs. Women who feel their bodies are repulsive and the source of evil in their lives make jokes about jiggly butts and sagging arm flesh. Humor makes us laugh at the most painful things in our lives, distracting us from the tragedy within the joke.

Overcoming our stories necessarily means revisiting old pain. Humor helps us do that if we can recognize it for what it is—an attempt to ameliorate anguish. If we use humor to be kind to ourselves, we might more easily be able to see the pain we've been in for so long, to see what contorted shapes we've twisted ourselves into simply to feel loved, recognized, and adequate.

Knowing When You're in a Defensive State

It would be so simple if we could just see when we're using one of these behaviors. But these roadblocks are devilish and highly skilled. Luckily, there are ways to know when we're in a defensive state. Here are some symptoms to suggest that the unconscious has armed itself and is trying to deflect our gazes from uncovering our stories:

- *Rigidity.* Our positions on something are entrenched.
- *The need to be right.* No matter how conciliatory the other person is being, we have to make sure they know we had the right answer or position.
- *An out-of-proportion reaction.* Something small happens and we blow our stacks.
- *An inappropriate reaction.* We laugh when we shouldn't, we cry when nothing's really wrong, or we lecture when it's not called for.
- *Numbness.* When something happens and we can't respond, we feel dead.
- *When certain situations totally exhaust us.* The mere thought of going to our in-laws' house, office, or parents' house completely depletes us.
- *Familiar feelings that may not connect to what's going on.* We have a sense of déjà vu but can't figure out why we feel something that

seems unconnected to the event that inspired it—like a sad feeling, reminiscent of a past sad event in the midst of a happy occasion.

- *Feeling strangely up or strangely down.* Manic emotions usually mean we're running away from something.
- *Feedback from one or more of our loved ones that we might be acting out.* More than one person asks what planet we're on. Frankly, if it walks like a duck and quacks like a duck, it's probably a duck. Listen to them—we're defending ourselves against some truth we'd rather not see.

Once we recognize we're in a defensive position, it leads us to the fact that what we're really defending is our stories. All the denials, projections, and self-destructive humor are wagons circled against a foe. Even though we've outgrown our need for our stories, even though they have stopped working for us and indeed are working against us, it still takes tremendous courage to take the step of disarming our defenses and looking our stories in the eye.

Tools for When You're Stuck

Because the story is unconscious, it's not at all surprising that we get stuck trying to go where our defenses don't want to let us wander. Sometimes we can see that we're in a defensive state, make the roadblock and its behavior conscious, and *still* not be able to see what the story is underneath that we're defending. Luckily, there are two powerful tools that can move us forward when we hit what we think are dead ends—dreamwork and free association.

Dreamwork

Dreams are a tremendous source of information because they reflect our wishes and conflicts. Dreams take an emotional situation and build a play around it. They have a logic all their own, and there's a big difference between what's in the dream and what those things can mean. Learning to interpret dreams helps tremendously because they can lead us to the source of our biggest conflicts. Some dreams are more transparent than others. There's the classic dream in which you have to take a test and some performance anxiety comes up. That one is simple to decode. But there can be other disturbing dreams, ones that people are often reluctant to think about, especially when the dream involves breaking a taboo. If we remember that in the dream-world we're dealing with symbols, we can begin to look at these symbols as data to further our understanding of ourselves, and not as a demonstration of something that offends or frightens us about ourselves or others.

There are an infinite number of dreams, but there are six dream themes that are extremely common—being naked, something happening with your teeth, being chased, flying, taking a test, and falling. The specific meaning for you depends on what is going on in your life, but these might help jump-start you when you can't figure out what the message is that you're receiving from your old story.

Dreams of Being Naked

It's not what it concretely seems—that you'll be embarrassed by showing up somewhere not in your clothes. This dream often symbolizes feelings of vulnerability or shame. The concept that you may be exposed in some way metaphorically is at the heart here. The question becomes what is going on in the dreamers' lives that they may be feeling that way about. Are they hiding something? Are they afraid people can see through them to something they don't want seen? This could be a mistake or a misjudgment that your peers may see something about which you are terribly insecure. Clothes conceal insecurities in our dreams. It could be that you are in a relationship and afraid to show your true feelings. Being naked also can mean getting caught off guard in some way—naked in a schoolroom or at work—and you feel unprepared or like a fraud. Sometimes in your dreams you may be walking around naked and no one notices. That may be reassuring you that whatever you're afraid of is going right by people. It could also be a wish to be noticed. If you're naked and fine about it, that could mean you are feeling strong and happy and secure with who you are.

Dreams About Problems with Teeth

Teeth falling out symbolizes not being able to hold on to someone, fears of being rejected, or having been sexually damaged in some way. Teeth also symbolize aggression and power—think of biting and gnashing. Therefore, losing teeth can signify feelings of powerlessness, lack of confidence, or inferiority. Women of menopausal age often dream of their teeth falling out, and this speaks of their fears about getting older and being less attractive or less sexually potent or feminine.

Dreams of Being Chased

Thematically, these are anxiety dreams of some imminent danger. If you are running away from something and can't seem to move, it may represent running away from something in your waking life or trying to avoid something you're afraid of. So the question is, Who is chasing you in the dream? Thinking about the who or the what may give you some insight into the source of your fear in waking life. It's also possible that the person who is chasing you is part of yourself, and the dream has something to do with something you fear from within— love or envy or behavior that you're indulging in that you know is not good for you.

Dreams of Flying

Flying in dreams can be positive or negative. Some flying dreams are quite dreadful experiences for the dreamer. In some dreams, you may be flying easily, looking down, and it may be exhilarating, being above everything and doing well. This can reflect a sense of personal power and control as you maneuver yourself. It also could be a wish that you had control over something you don't. It may represent a struggle to stay in control, or it could be about an obstacle in your life or a person who is standing in your way. Think about what it is in your dream that is standing in your way, and it may be representative of something in waking life.

Flying can also represent a fear of and a wish for success—you're flying too high in the dream; you're afraid of the challenge of success.

Dreams About Tests/Performances

Taking a test you're not prepared for, performing in a concert on an instrument you don't know how to play, or acting in a play and you don't know the lines are classic anxiety dreams. These dreams are about the feeling that something is testing you in your life that has to do with overall self-esteem and confidence. These dreams can indicate that you are worried that you aren't measuring up to other people's expectations of you. It could mean you feel you aren't acceptable. You may feel unprepared for some challenge that's coming up in life. But this is usually about feeling inadequate about your abilities and not about the content of the test.

Sometimes a test dream indicates you've passed a test in life or have gone beyond an expectation.

Dreams About Falling

This is an insecurity dream about feeling overwhelmed or insecure or out of control in your life. It may have to do with a relationship or something at work, that feeling you can't hang on or keep up with what's going on. This dream may also have to do with a sense of failure in some situation—in a love relationship or at work that somehow you aren't measuring up. Look for places in your life where you're feeling inadequate.

Free Association

This tool is classically used in any kind of analysis, but you don't need a therapist to benefit from it. It is allowing the mind to wander freely from thought to thought without censoring *anything*. Say you know you are in a situation where your story is directing you. You know this because you are having a huge reaction to something that isn't all that important, and you are pointing blame at everyone around you. In other words, you're using all your favorite defenses. But, for the life of you, you can't figure out which old story is creating all the internal chaos.

Remove yourself from the situation (remember, think don't act) and ask yourself these questions:

- What first comes to mind when you think of this situation?
- Who does this remind you of?
- What situation in your past does this remind you of?
- What relationship does this feel like?
- What objects or people pop up?
- Make a note to yourself as you float around in thought. Then come back later and look at each object or person.

I used these questions with Pat, who was about to become a grand-mother for the first time but wasn't happy about it. Her lack of enthu-siasm made her feel like a bad person, and, Perfectionist that she was, she had become quite depressed. I asked her these questions. Her situ-ation didn't really remind her of anyone or anything, but for some rea-son, candlesticks popped into her head. She wrote it down. Now, thinking back on the candlesticks, the next thing that came to her mind was Thanksgiving. She was immediately flooded with sadness. It was during a Thanksgiving dinner that her grandmother had collapsed and gone to the hospital where she ultimately died. Pat could make the connection between her current situation and her unresolved grief about her grandmother. She could connect her sadness about her grand-mother's loss to her first fears about death, including fears of her own mortality. But she could do more than that. Her grandmother had raised her with very strict moral dicta. Pat had become a Perfectionist under her watchful eye. Her grandmother ultimately held the key to Pat's whole story.

This tool will always lead you somewhere that has meaning. But to use it properly, you have to take some time. It's hard for people in this day and age to sit still and spend time letting their minds wander when it's become so easy to just take a pill and feel better. We don't make it a priority to give ourselves time to lie on our beds or sit on our sofas to let our minds wander. It's also difficult not to censor our thoughts to avoid feeling scared or "bad." Allowing awareness of *all* thoughts is the cornerstone of free association.

One final note about free association. What comes out of your thoughts may be very primitive memories. You may feel very sad or angry. This is natural, and if you stick with the feelings, they will lead you to your story's messages. But because the work is deep, you need to give yourself some time for "reentry," so don't do this right before you go to bed. Take time in the morning or afternoon. If you want, use a journal to record your thoughts. I had one patient who used a tape recorder to note where her mind wandered. Give yourself adequate time to go deeply and come out completely.

The Therapeutic Process

Sometimes we hit messages that are too difficult to decode or too overwhelming. If you feel immobilized—can't get out of bed, can't function at work, can't reach out to loved ones, don't want to eat—by sadness, depression, or anxiety, please get some professional help. Even if you aren't having a severe reaction, you may find that working with a psychoanalyst or psychotherapist accelerates your process. Also, depression and anxiety can grow to where they impair the judgment you need to do this work. If depression or anxiety is interfering with your ability to function, you may require medication to lift these feelings so that you can work on your stories. Severe depression and anxiety can be lethal, so if you feel hopeless and overwhelmed, get an evaluation by a trained professional.

Living Consciously

Nothing is more important in your journey to being real than being consciously aware. Now that you are aware of the kinds of defenses you use that can be roadblocks to change, you can make conscious choices about what you do in response to life's complexities. Living consciously requires vigilance—we need to be self-aware and honest. We need to keep our minds prioritized on rooting out the messages of our old stories and focusing instead on the new, rewritten ones. Each time we act on our new instructions, we strengthen our new stories. Conscious living means we will be aware of when we are trying to revert to old ways and when we take cover in the responses of our old personalities. Conscious living means we will regress, deny, and try to block changes, but we will try to know it. Most of all, conscious living means we have to learn to live with and indeed *embrace* emotional discomfort and pain because we now know that it leads to getting rid of behaviors and messages we no longer need in our lives—the very messages that hold us back from being the real, huge, rich, authentic selves we in fact are right now.

Chapter Fourteen

BEING REAL

I'm often asked, "How will I know when I'm no longer living in a story?" Because the story was so invisible when it governed our lives, it's hard to picture how we will recognize its absence. Luckily, living consciously in our adult realities is a bit like an orgasm—hard to imagine but not hard to miss once you've had one. There are a few properties of being real we all get to enjoy—no matter what the specifics of our lives are. We know we're real when:

- We're able to see how many choices we have and feel free to consider our options.
- We can feel ambivalently about those we love and still be able to feel love and be even more intimate with them.
- We feel safe enough to be curious about what's working and what's not working in our lives.

- We have a greater understanding of who we are and why we feel what we feel.
- We suffer less with frustration, depression, or anxiety, and we can be aware of those feelings, accepting them as part of our lives.
- We are able to stop acting reflexively in a self-destructive, obsessive, or defensive way.
- We can see great variety in the possibilities of outcomes instead of feeling condemned to repeat unwanted situations or behaviors.
- We stop having repetitive outbursts that always lead us back to the same place.
- We accept that life is hard sometimes, and while there is struggle, the effort holds great promise.
- It doesn't feel so risky to love others, to give of ourselves, to start down new generative paths, and to try things that we've been too frightened to try before.
- Overall, we suffer less and enjoy life more. We find more peace and contentment.

I recognize that this is quite a list, but it's remarkable how consistent these properties are. When we are no longer defending against loss or fear, we free ourselves from the restrictions imposed.

Desperation had made Sydney more open-minded. She started to see that there might be more than one way to interpret her actions. She started to see herself through Brian's eyes and admitted to me that her erratic and controlling behavior didn't look so good to him. The realization stunned her into inaction, which for her was a very good thing even if it left her temporarily depressed and scared. She started to understand that what she thought she was shielding Brian from—her neediness, her dependence—actually pushed him away. More than that, she saw how second nature those behaviors were. Even though she understood intellectually that her personality had its roots in abandonment—her father's departure and mother's depression—that understanding alone had meant very little to her.

But when Sydney finally understood that she'd taken that initial abandonment and preserved it by making it the core of her Dependent personality, she felt ready to move beyond old behavior. She got some traction on her slippery life.

Gradually, Sydney tried telling Brian what she was feeling before she "shielded" him from it. She told him what she was scared of or when she wanted attention. The more she practiced saying what she needed, the less frightening it was and the easier it became. Brian didn't run away. In fact, he was so overjoyed at being needed, even Sydney could see what a gift she was giving him as she revealed her "real" self to him. Slowly, that pretzel shape unfolded, and Sydney could make an intimate connection with someone who loved her very much.

The Gifts of Reality: Curiosity and Generativity

As we move beyond the limits of our childhood stories, we experience a security we haven't felt before that allows our horizons to expand in all directions. One of the first gifts we receive is that of curiosity. One hidden cost of our stories is that they inhibit exploration and spontaneity—two key components of curiosity. It's very common that stories discourage curiosity because curiosity skirts the edge between taboo and knowledge. As kids, one of the leading things we wonder about is our parents and their sex lives. While this is completely natural and essential to our growth, our society sometimes mishandles our cues to our kids and either oversexualizes situations or equates sex with something shameful. When that happens, these emotions lead us over the line and form the center of a story. This happened with Phil, who, as a child, walked into his parents' bedroom while they were having sex. Phil's father was stunned and upset. He yelled for his son to get out of the room and never enter again without knocking. Because his father felt so embarrassed, he did not discuss it in any way with Phil. He acted angry, and he was angry with himself for not locking the door, but Phil felt that the anger was directed at him. His father treated it in a way that made Phil feel terribly guilty—as if it were his fault. When something like this happens, a child can develop a story that it's bad to be curious—that wanting to know is what got them into trouble and makes them morally bad.

A lack of curiosity affects all kinds of things—from learning to socializing. As we've seen, a little can go a very long way in the unconscious. Until that story is rewritten, any kind of exploration can be very anxiety provoking. I have one patient who never goes to parties precisely because she is afraid to meet new people. Not because she's shy. She says she just doesn't want to know anyone else. Her anxiety becomes overwhelming because, in fact, she *is* intensely curious about others but feels this is bad, and so rather than stir her curiosity, she avoids anything that might whet her appetite.

But when we expose this tale, something wonderful results. Our worlds enlarge almost overnight. We learn new things about old friends, perhaps things they think we always knew but were afraid to see. We can embrace nuance and ambiguity because neither reflects on us anymore. It's as if, when we sever the causal connection that says "curiosity = bad," we turn on the lights in a room we've been standing in for years.

The second gift we get when we become real is generatitivy. When I speak of "generativity," I mean the ability to create new things—whether it's making a baby, starting a new relationship, or developing new interests in life. It's very hard to be generative when we're afraid. Creativity involves risk and vulnerability. By definition, we have to open ourselves up to new ideas and emotions—many of which we may have been unconsciously guarding against. When we live in that defended state—and all stories keep us in one—we have a hard time creating.

Some of us are trapped by the story that says there's something dangerous about generating. It can spring from something as unconscious and simple as sibling rivalry—we watch our mothers' growing belly with both excitement about the new baby and fear we're going to be replaced. Perhaps there's a big age gap between us and this new baby. Suddenly, we have to move over, which gets folded into our concept of generating new things. Creating equals displacement. Therefore, creating anything new—whether a new life or a new career—may be a very conflicted process. And conflict creates anxiety, and our stories are built to reduce anxiety. Thus, we bury this conflict under our personalities, sealing in our ambivalence for the rest of our lives unless it is exposed.

This fear of generativity particularly applies when people get older. Many women lose the feeling of creativity because they no longer can have children. Maybe they're widowed or their careers are ending or they've retired. They've lost the feeling they can make something new of their lives. When we are real, we may experience the sadness that can come with the end of our childbearing years. Retirement might depress us. But what we don't feel is that we are used up and have nothing left to generate. Instead, we can separate out the function from the person and be as creative as we wish. When we expose our stories, we find that we have the strength and equilibrium to carry us through the unsettling emotions of grief, loss, and depression. They no longer act as guardians at the door of our lives.

Sometimes I hear from "creative" people with substance problems that they're afraid that if they stop drinking or using drugs they will no longer be good writers/actors/painters. This is the story in full flower. They feel the excess opens them up and is the source of their creativity. I have seen quite the opposite. There's a big difference between the lowered inhibitions that a stiff round of drinks creates and the powerful energy that bursts on the scene when it's no longer put to use defending a story. Imagine how much more they can accomplish when both hands are free to create the dreams from their imaginations instead of having one hand occupied with propping up their stories.

The Promises of a Real Life

Nature abhors a vacuum. When we cease certain behaviors, new ones take their place. It's important to know that when we rewrite our stories, we don't change who we are. But we do minimize our conflicted feelings and stop being *compelled* to act in certain ways. When we, as adults, can hold up our actions to the light of day and see that what's motivating them is old and outdated, we have so many more choices. There's no longer *one* job or *one* man. There's no longer only *one* right way. We no longer need the rigidity that made us feel safe. When it dissolves, we get much larger lives.

There are five important gifts you will acquire from living a real life. Each results when we rewrite our stories, and they apply to everyone:

- Authenticity
- Personal Freedom

- True Strength
- Self-acceptance (all-inclusive, positive and negative)
- Intimacy (an ability to be truly intimate with others)

Authenticity

When we stop putting up false fronts—even well-motivated ones—authenticity naturally results. When you no longer have to build a buffer between who you fear you are and what you present to the world, you experience a tremendous freedom. Everyone who comes into my office in the beginning has the feeling to some degree that they're a fake or fraud and that they have to constantly pedal hard to pretend to be something they feel they are not. There's a difference between being nice to someone you don't really like because you're afraid of the repercussions of not being nice and being nice because it's the politically astute thing to do. In the first case, your fear rules the day, and in the second, you make the decision based on conscious feelings. Your actions may look the same on the outside, but inside, you've made a decision that is in alignment with who you are and what you need to do. When you're nice out of fear, it's because your story has you acting out an old drama that isn't even present but one that still compels you. Inside there's a world of difference. You're in control of your choices, and they are made based on who you are today, not what worried you years ago. Authenticity is knowing who we are today and acting from that understanding.

Personal Freedom

Personal freedom is a huge part of being real. It springs from our authenticity. When we know ourselves for who we are, we feel secure and are less inhibited about trying new and different things. That freedom can express itself in the relationship arena where we find ourselves saying, "I'm going to try to be more myself, ask for what I want. I feel free to ask for more or stick my toe in the water more fully because it doesn't feel so dangerous." This freedom extends to our work as well—we encourage ourselves to take chances, stretch, be more creative. We can do this in part because we have stopped constantly criticizing ourselves and saying things like "What if they misunderstand what I'm trying to do? I can't take that chance, so I'm not going to do it." With personal freedom you end up feeling that your well-being or success isn't conditional. You are okay just as you are. This recognition allows you to feel angry or take chances, try something on for size. Trying new things is incredibly exhilarating.

True Strength

When we stop guarding ourselves, we get personal freedom—freedom in relationships, freedom in taking risks, freedom in pursuing difficult things in life even though we might fail. When we see ourselves clearly for the adults we are, we can look at how much we have accomplished in our lives. Remembering to treat ourselves with empathy, we can see that even in places where we have fallen short of our hopes, we were still able to contribute, achieve, and enjoy. But when we are authentic, and are free to express who we are, it results in feeling really capable. We believe we can handle whatever life tosses us, and life *will* toss us difficult things. Children are vulnerable and helpless. Our stories trap us and keep us childlike. Moving beyond them releases those frozen, immature aspects that needed the crutch of the fictions, and results in the wonderful self-confidence of adulthood.

Self-acceptance

When we're in our stories, we live with blame. We blame ourselves; we blame others. Things are unacceptable. We always feel critical of ourselves and others. We rail that life is unfair. We blame when we feel like we are helpless or powerless victims. But being real, knowing who we are, knowing what we like and don't like allows us to say, "I don't like this. I can choose to do something about it." Or we can recognize with unblinded eyes that sometimes life just hands us hard and even unfair burdens. That's the way life is. But there's a huge difference between something undesired being unacceptable and its being unwanted or unpleasant. We get to choose how we respond to life, not what life presents us. Accepting what we're given doesn't make us passive; it saves us from the slavery of misery and helpless whining. Acceptance allows us to choose our battles and decide how to handle what we're given.

When we accept ourselves for who we are, we widen the channel through which strength, creativity, and intimacy flow. Self-criticism blocks that artery with boulders of self-recrimination. When we accept others for who they are, it gives us a starting ground for creating real relationships.

Intimacy

As we've discussed throughout the book, if you are unable to be honest with yourself, you certainly can't be honest with someone else. Without that honesty, you won't be able to communicate with the other person and let them really know you. If you aren't really yourself with another person, there is only so much intimacy you can have.

When you are less critical of yourself and your loved ones, it creates trust and closeness that are the cornerstones of intimacy. When we're accepting of ourselves and others, we can handle ambivalent feelings about our loved ones. Those feelings always exist in every relationship. But when we feel secure in our adult selves, we can handle those mixed feelings and speak up for how we feel. We don't have to pretend those feelings aren't there and hide ourselves away. You can say, "Hey, Stanley, please take a shower before we have sex because you don't smell good," instead of holding your nose—and yourself back—then having sex with Stanley and resenting him for it. This intimacy—this I see you and you see me—represents the fulfillment of our primary emotional needs as we are recognized for our true selves. We are no longer slaves to the need to be connected to love or be crushed. We can choose to be with people who love us for who we are.

When Others Are Not Real

One of the repercussions of seeing your story and how it operates in your daily life is that other people's stories will become visible to you. It's also always easier when you are standing outside to be more objective about somebody else's stuff. Even if it pushes your buttons, it's still easier than being in your own head. Now that you know what to look for, though, you will start seeing people's stories everywhere. Your natural inclination is going to be to try to help them see their own messages and personalities and defenses. This is dicey business, because chances are, they are as defended as you were. You have to proceed slowly.

The best way to help others always is to lead by example. When you start making changes that are visible to other people around you, they're going to see them and say, "Hey what's going on?" That's an opportunity for you to say, "I've become introspective lately, and I've thought about who I am and have made some changes. Maybe this would be helpful for you, too." With people you are very close to— your spouse, kids, friends—if something comes up and it's a repetitive pattern, you can collect a few examples of things you've seen. Try to pick ones that are not highly critical because it's always hard for people to hear criticism. If they feel too judged, they're going to be defensive and turn you off. The best way to make people conscious of their repetitive and destructive patterns is by showing them the ways they're being self-sabotaging rather than by telling them what they're doing to you. As soon as you start saying, "You're doing this to me," they're going to summon their defenses. Instead, try to gently note a few things you can see from afar that they're doing to themselves. Take Lisa, for instance, who was eating and drinking too much because she was angry at her father. Because she was so highly tuned to his judgment, he was almost powerless to help her. But he can say what he has to say by being loving: "Honey, I love you. I see you eating too much, which I know in the end makes you unhappy because I know you are self-conscious about your weight. It seems to me that it's really self-destructive. I wonder if you can ask yourself what's going on."

As I've said a million times in my practice, you can only lead the horse to water. Somebody has to make the choice to take the drink. If you love someone, you'll try. You don't have to give up. But you don't have to drive people nuts either. You can try to point out behaviors, and sometimes people just can't hear it the first time. But if you catch them a month later with a different version of the behavior going on, you can try to point it out again as long as you're not up in their faces with "I told you so" but instead with "This reminds me of these other things, and because I love you, I'd love to see you help yourself." Even defensive people will hear this sooner or later.

Sometimes people aren't going to like the changes you've made. But this work of being real isn't about pleasing other people—that's a story you can get stuck in. I'm not suggesting everyone go out and ignore the feelings of those around them. This process is about gaining contentment and self-satisfaction. In the end that should include trying to be good to those you love—that's part of self-satisfaction. But we do have patterns of behavior with people that are going to change. Be patient while those around you readjust to the real you. They may have wanted to see these changes you've made for years, but any change is still unsettling.

Sometimes people will not like the real you. Say you've had the personality of a Competitor all these years, and you've acted the part of a sex kitten. Now you actually feel safer not wearing the heels and the form-fitting clothes. Your boyfriend looks at you and says, "What happened to the girl in the miniskirt?" Well, that may not be the boyfriend you want. But sometimes the answers are unexpected. He may be kind of relieved—after all, he may say, "Whew, it was lot of pressure for me to have been 'phallic man' to your sex kitten. This is relaxing." He may even point out that without your more narrow story, there's even more to you to find terrific.

How people respond depends on who you've picked to be in your life. If that person's sharply in alignment with your story, you might outgrow them. That happens all the time, as unfortunate and as sad as it can be. I have people who come into therapy, do the work of becoming real, and one of two things happens: They grow and their partners simply aren't going to do the same work. When this happens, they do ultimately surpass their loved ones and decide they have to move on. Or they're growing and their partner sees the changes and wants to come along and grow, too. There's no formula and no predictions. Just be patient and conscious and let the changes have a chance to settle in before you uproot anything in your life.

A Lifelong Journey

Being real is a lifelong journey. It isn't about "you've read this book in two weeks and now you're done." What really goes on inside is the process of maturing. I'm trying to help people have adult stories grounded in the grown-ups they are today. Sydney's more mature story recognizes that Brian is her boyfriend, soon-to-be husband, and not her father. She has to be able to see her situation with adult eyes and understand that she's neither a helpless little girl nor a shrew like her mother. Instead, she's a grown woman with an awful lot to offer. When she's conscious of her story and personality type, she can see that her story will cause her to turn all men into her father and treat them as she would a man who might leave at any moment. When she is conscious of that, she can maturely see this isn't true of Brian. Looking at her relationship with adult eyes allows her to give of herself and to see that she has enough good in her that someone will want to stick around.

Generally speaking, this process doesn't work like a cartoon lightbulb. You probably aren't going to have one of those "AHA" experiences and awaken the next morning to find that everything has changed.

But you will find that your core story dissipates over time. It gradually withers in the face of your real adult presence.

But be prepared: Your story has tendrils. Sydney sees that Brian is not her father, but she's got other areas where she's applied that story—at work, in friendships. Her story isn't isolated, and she's built much of who she is on its foundations. Sydney may find, as you do, that she still has plenty of old behaviors—ones that compel her to be the most accommodating negotiator at every business meeting or physically collapsing to get attention. These are things that dissolve over time. We all need to keep proving to ourselves that we are strong and capable and deserving of love. As we do, we discover more mature ways to operate in the world.

Often our stories reignite during critical milestones—childbirth, menopause, death. I tell Sydney that one day if she has kids, she might just lose her temper and yell at them. Her old story's reaction would be to worry that her kids aren't going to love her because she yelled. But kids need to know their parents are only human, and sometimes humans can yell when they're pissed off. So she is going to have to catch herself and realize she just got a message from an old story. Hopefully at that point, she'll be able to say, "Wait a minute, it's okay not to be the perfect parent. They will love me anyway." She may even be able to tell them she wished she hadn't yelled but be able to calmly explain why she became angry with them.

When we can catch ourselves and become conscious, we're given a whole new way of being. We're able to choose what to do. This awareness of our old default positions will give us choices that will inform everything we do—from how we pick partners to how we respond to life's milestones. When you know your personality style, you know how you're likely to respond and what your weak or blind spots are. But you also know your strengths, grounded in your mature self. This ensures that you can ride through life's real challenges and losses with the flexibility required to make the most of your life.

The time comes for all of us when we lose our parents, and that is a most difficult transition. It makes us think about mortality, that we're next in line, that we're no longer somebody's child. We don't want to go through this passage of our lives and regret the opportunities lost to personalities formed of fear, hurt, or loss. These extraordinarily difficult passages in life are made much easier when they aren't experienced through the narrow prism of the immature child's story.

As you live your real life, be patient with yourself, because this is a new way of thinking. What starts in one little area may grow larger than you imagined. The point is to evolve into a new way of thinking that will become more second nature the more you practice telling yourself your old story and rewriting it. I hope this is just the beginning of a life filled with understanding, opportunity, and self-fulfillment . . . a life of being real.

ACKNOWLEDGMENTS

The person I feel most thankful to and for is my husband, Lenny, whose endless encouragement, support, smart advice, humor, and love have been truly instrumental in my writing this book. The best experiences of my life have been raising with him our three fantastic children, and those experiences have been truly revealing in the understanding of my own stories. My children have also been supportive and proud of what I do, making the work on this book all the more enjoyable. Thank you, girls!

I could never sufficiently thank Liz Perle, an extraordinarily gifted writer as well as a highly intelligent and lovely person. Her sharp intuition about others and her psychological mindedness have made her an invaluable person to work with.

Many thank-yous to Marly Rusoff, who believed in me, gave me my chance, and saw me through when I had never authored a book.

Thank you for being so smart, so upbeat, so accessible, so encouraging, and so hardworking.

My gratitude goes to Amy Hertz, my editor, who proved the point that real improvement cannot be gotten without first going through some pain. I thank her for making this a much better book, for having a vision and great sense of organization, and for dealing kindly with a nervous first author. Also thanks to Marc Haeringer for always answering my many questions with patience and politeness.

Thank you to my brother, Adam, and my sister, Holly, who read early versions of this work and gave me wonderful ideas and loads of support. Thank you for always sticking by me and for being so important to me. Thank you to my parents who have remained my lifelong "objective" fans and believed that I could do this and do it well. Mom and Dad, I have always appreciated your great enthusiasm for my endeavors. No matter how "out there" my ideas have seemed, you have always encouraged my attempts, sympathized when I fell, and cheered when I succeeded.

I really want to thank my friends who have cheered me on, have advised me well, and have been patient and empathic when I was scared, but always stuck by me with their love and encouragement. Thank you Mikey, Erica, Nate, Nancy, Liza, Kevin, Lori, Terri, and Ann.

I am indebted to the wonderful people at NBC's *Today* show, especially Cheryl and Betsy, and at *Glamour* magazine for the opportunity to speak to the public about issues of mental health, something that I believe is of huge importance and that I truly love doing. A special thank-you to Katie Couric for her friendship and her understanding of and interest in all issues psychological. Also, thanks to Dottie Jeffries for her support and great ideas in the arena of public education.

Acknowledgments

I could not do the work I do without the wonderful training I have received from many teachers and supervisors at The New York Psychoanalytic Institute. In particular, I would like to thank Dr. Ronda Shaw, Dr. Leon Hoffman, Dr. Eslee Samberg, Dr. Edward Nersessian, and Dr. Herb Wyman for sharing their expertise and wisdom with me.

Last, but certainly not least, this book could not have been written without the many patients whose confidentiality I have promised to keep and who have taught me so much about courage, struggle, perseverance, strength, and becoming real.

INDEX